THE NEWCASTLE GUIDE TO
HEALING WITH CRYSTALS

THE NEWCASTLE GUIDE TO
HEALING WITH CRYSTALS

Balancing the Human Energy Field
For Physical and Spiritual Well-Being

PAMELA CHASE
&
JONATHAN PAWLIK

NEWCASTLE PUBLISHING CO., INC.
North Hollywood, California
1988

Edited by Jim Strohecker and Nancy Shaw
Cover/Book Design by Riley K. Smith and Teri Stewart
Illustrations by Nell Blackwell

First Edition May 1988

Grateful acknowledgement is made to the following for permission to
reprint copyrighted material:

Mystic Crystal Publications: Excerpts from "Counseling With
    Crystals," by Judith Larkin, Ph.D., in *The Crystal Sourcebook*, John
    Vincent Milewski and Virginia L. Hanford, eds. Copyright 1987 by
    Mystic Crystal Publications.

A Newcastle Book
First Printing May 1988
9   8   7   6   5   4   3
Printed in the United States of America

ACKNOWLEDGEMENTS

We lovingly acknowledge and thank Katryn LaVanture and Karen Williams for their special support, as well as our other friends in Harrisburg, Pennsylvania, who have shared their crystal experiences and their personal journeys with us.

We give special thanks to the fine people at Newcastle Publishing for their talents in birthing this book.

Finally, we thank the crystals who have patiently taught us so much.

DISCLAIMER

This book is not intended to diagnose, prescribe, or treat any ailment, nor is it intended in any way as a replacement for medical consultation when needed. The author and publishers of this book do not guarantee the efficacy of any of the methods herein described, and strongly suggest that at the first suspicion of any disease or disorder the reader consult a physician.

CONTENTS

List of Illustrations

INTRODUCTION

Prominent among the crystals in my personal collection is a huge, single-pointed beauty with six sides sitting on a flat base. When I dare to think of its birth and the eons of time which have passed during its journey from its natural origins to the comfortable library shelf it presently calls home, I am in awe. Still, I find it difficult to grasp the full concept of its nature. The vital and compelling energy of crystal, as well as its inherent healing qualities, perpetually exists in its living presence. Containing the "God Essence," it radiates a unique and beneficial power that man is just now rediscovering.

In this book Pamela Chase and Jonathan Pawlik give a sensitive introduction to the ancient and modern use of crystals as tools for spiritual, mental, and physical healing. The authors offer a new mode of interpretation for the study of crystals. They reveal a clear, simple, and effective process for learning which provides both techniques and practical applications. Their unique and relaxing style gives the reader a warm and enlightening experience. While sitting in my den reading this book, I felt that I could hear the "stone-person" (Jonathan) discussing the qualities and uses of the various crystals. Sitting opposite in the large leather chair, I could see the "plant-person" (Pamela) handling the crystals lovingly as they both brought the book to life.

I hope the reader will use this book to further expand his or her knowledge. A broad path is presented here by the authors. This path allows the reader to explore the fascinating world of crystals. Many in-depth works have been written on the special aspects and uses of crystal. There is so much currently known and so much still unknown about crystals that no one book can encompass the subject. This book is a good key for unlocking the door of the reader's curiosity about the mystery of crystal healing.

In recent years the research of esoteric scholars has gradually removed the dust of ages which had obscured the ancient knowledge of crystals. Consequently, we are now being exposed to the powerful and forgotten healing therapies associated with the quartz crystal. Various esoteric procedures are being improved upon by the additional power of the quartz crystal. Crystal energy is being utilized in the development of exciting new techniques for healing and consciousness expansion. Its potential uses are vast and diverse. Esoteric scholars are now finding that each type of crystal has its own unique vibratory energy, and that each vibratory energy has its corresponding individual properties. The current use of crystals represents yet another significant revival of an ancient esoteric science.

Acquiring your first crystal can be an exciting and time-consuming endeavor. Many people feel compelled to buy a crystal because of its beauty and apparent magnetism. This is meaningful! If you are strongly drawn or attracted to a crystal, I feel this is sufficient reason to make your decision.

It has been written that the crystal was used profusely in Atlantis. The many ways it was used, however, have not yet been fully revealed. Now it appears that Atlanteans are in the process of coming together once again! Could this be the reason why you are a crystal enthusiast? I wonder. Could this be the reason why you are filling your personal bookshelf with books about crystals? Are you beginning to open up to past knowledge? Are you looking for the key? These somewhat provocative questions may alert your present-day consciousness to a hidden well of knowledge which you brought with you in this lifetime. Consider these things—your own interest may uncover yet another valuable part of the magnificent crystal puzzle.

There is a deep sense of order and tranquility in this work, which I feel is a welcome contribution to the ever-expanding knowledge of crystals. At this point I am tempted to draw upon a metaphor from music. Imagine if you will, a Twentieth Century Esoteric Symphony of Life. This book could be then seen as a "variation on a theme" which allows us to "see" and "hear" a *Crystal Healing Overture* through the sensitive and harmonious efforts of Pamela Chase and Jonathan Pawlik.

Eileen Connolly
February 9, 1988

PREFACE

Jonathan is a "stone person." Stone people often had rock collections when they were children and loved to browse on beaches collecting shells and beautiful pebbles. They may carry stones in their pockets for "good luck." While walking in the forest they love to intently examine the smooth rocks in the bottom of stream beds. If you show them your precious gemstone jewelry their eyes light up with excitement, as they are probably collectors as well. Jonathan's natural interest and love of minerals was given a new focus some years ago when he was exposed to books on the metaphysical and healing properties of gemstones.

I, on the other hand, am a "plant person." Trees, wildflowers and gardens are a major source of comfort and inspiration for me. In the beginning it was hard for me to sense the energies of crystals. Jonathan would hand me a crystal and say, "Do you sense the quiet energy?" and I would respond, "I don't feel anything." Frustration would build up inside. Gradually, with Jonathan's loving patience, I learned how to sense subtle energies, with the crystals acting as the catalyst in the process. *The Newcastle Guide to Healing with Crystals* describes our growth with this unique mineral and the ways that we personalized our relationship with crystals. Our book is also about healing. My search for understanding and peace of mind has been through the heart, with years of therapy, peer counseling, and learning from life-changing experiences. The fruit of all that work seems to be an understanding and application of the healing process which can be shared with others.

Our marriage has also been about healing. This book was born of our creative energies and a desire to be of service to others. The process of conceiving this book has been unique. First, Jonathan would receive channeled information and then we would integrate the new knowledge into our healing and counseling work. Our process has been to learn step by step. This has allowed us to develop our intuitive skills in such a way that we can teach it to others.

The material in the text which is in ''quotes'' and in this typeface has been channeled through Jonathan by the Crystal Devas and from the guides that work with him. Every living thing in creation has an evolving Consciousness which is part of the greater Consciousness that we call God. Your *Higher Self* is that part of your Consciousness that is aware of its connection with God and can be contacted as a spiritual advisor. You are a particular form or aspect of your Godself, living on Planet Earth to learn a particular set of lessons about the greater Consciousness.

Devas are the "Higher Selves" for the Kingdoms of Nature. They are the architects for the physical forms that we see. Because they are not separate from the greater Consciousness or God, they are teachers of love and understanding. The Kingdoms of Nature evolve through giving love and service just as we do. The Kingdoms of Nature wish to work with us in a co-creative capacity, which requires a radical shift in our current state of awareness.

We have come to better understand that each one of us receives information in different ways and we incorporate those perceptions into our own belief systems. Therefore, there is *no right way* to work with crystals. What we share here is our own experience, and you can incorporate what is relevant into your own ways of working and perceiving. Do not assume that if we say something that contradicts your own perceptions, it means that one of us is "wrong." Trust your perceptions and know that you are guided in your own process of learning as we all are. This process takes patience and practice, and we hope you will learn to see crystals and other forms of life with new eyes.

Pamela Chase

THE NEWCASTLE GUIDE TO
HEALING WITH CRYSTALS

PART ONE

Understanding Quartz Crystals

1 | The Crystal Bridge To Personal Transformation

THE GREEK WORD for crystal, *krystallos*, means "clear ice." We don't know whether the concept of "solidified ice" was their literal or their metaphorical understanding. However, we do know that the term "krystallos" originally referred only to clear quartz crystal. In time the term was applied in a more general way to any solid, symmetrical mineral, transparent or opaque, bounded by plane surfaces. Thus ruby, sapphire, amethyst, and other minerals came to be called crystals. In this book we focus our attention only on *natural, clear quartz crystal*, as its special properties give it more versatility then any other mineral. When we use the term "crystal" in this book, we are referring to clear quartz crystal.

In this chapter we will become acquainted with the crystal by first looking at some of its physical properties and uses. Then we will examine the "spiritual properties" of crystals, which are those qualities that cannot be measured scientifically.

PHYSICAL PROPERTIES OF CRYSTAL AND ITS USES IN TECHNOLOGY

Clear quartz crystal consists of molecules of silicon dioxide arranged in a highly structured geometric pattern. The molecules of silicon and oxygen are surrounded by a relatively vast open space which can be compressed and expanded by certain stimuli, or, in other words, made to *vibrate*. It is through this property that vibratory energies of different frequencies can be *stored* in crystals. Scientists have used crystals to store sound, light, and electrical frequencies in computers.

The crystal's highly ordered structure has the ability to be constant, coherent and reliable in its energy vibrations. For this reason, radio, television and other devices have their frequency controlled and directed by crystal oscillators. This may also be the reason why crystals are used to *focus* energy in lasers.

If you tap a crystal with a mallet, you can observe a brief flash of visible light, demonstrating the *piezoelectric* (pī ē′ zo) property of crystals. This property enables the crystal to *transform* a mechanical pressure into another form of energy such as light, electricity, or sound and then to *amplify* it. In a record player, for example, the needle is connected to a crystal element and rides in the record grooves. As the needle fluctuates, the mechanical stresses are connected to an electrical signal which is then amplified into sound.

Clear quartz crystal is used in the optical lenses of precision equipment because of its ability to *transmit* a greater range of the light spectrum with less distortion than glass. Therefore, we can see that crystal has the proven capabilities of *storing, focusing, transmitting, transforming,* and *amplifying* energy.

LIFE FORCE ENERGY AND THE ENERGY OF THOUGHT

We have looked at the properties of the crystal in terms of energy that can be measured. Now we will expand our definition of energy and take a look at its "spiritual properties." Once we begin to look at *reality as an energy system*, we are better able to understand the spiritual properties of crystal and its use in healing and consciousness expansion.

Physicists Albert Einstein and Nikola Tesla said that we are surrounded by a "sea of energy" which they described as invisible, boundless, and in perfect order. Physicists now define it as *zero point* energy: the energy which exists prior to its materialization in form. This energy has been described by a number of earlier scientists. Mesmer called it *animal magnetism*, Reich called it *orgone*, and the 18th century scientist Baron von Reichenbach called it *odic force*. This energy was called *prana* in the Hindu tradition and *chi* in the Chinese tradition. It has been described in the eastern spiritual traditions as *pure Consciousness*. In this book we will call it *life force energy*, the "raw stuff" out of which we are made.

On the physical level, life force energy ultimately becomes matter. On the spiritual level, life force energy becomes pure Consciousness. When we feel a sense of infinite joy, peace, and love, we are experiencing the spiritual aspect of life force energy.

Life force energy is also known to have *healing qualities*. The Chinese system of acupuncture is based on the flow of *chi* energy through the body. The ancient Indian system of Ayurvedic medicine utilizes *prana* as a healing force. The simple truth is that if we are able to incorporate more life force energy into our being on all levels, we will be healthier, happier, and more spiritually attuned. In healing work we are essentially transforming the unmanifested life force energy into manifestations of energy that can nourish and promote our well-being.

Using the analogy of life force energy as a "sea of energy," we are now ready to introduce the first of three key concepts to understanding the function of energy in healing: *Thoughts are a form of life force energy.* This idea has appeared in many forms throughout the world for thousands of years. In the Bible it is stated, "In the beginning was the Word, and the Word was with God, and the Word was God" (John 1:1). The original "Word" represents the absolute, focused creative power of Divine Energy. In comparison, our normal everyday thoughts lack this special focused power. We can describe our mundane, fleeting thoughts as weakly organized life force energy patterns that register like tiny ripples in this "sea" and then disappear. On the other hand, the additional force of focused will or strong feeling adds structure and energy to thought, creating a *thought form.* This thought form can be described as a specific patterned energy field which perpetuates itself as a continuous wave in our "sea of energy."

I had an awesome experience of the power of thought several years ago in which I was able to dissolve small clouds in the sky with a concentrated thought form or visualization. I got this visualization exercise from Richard Bach's book, *Illusions.* The first time I tried it, I sat down outside and chose a small group of clouds in the sky to which I could direct my thoughts. I visualized a hot laser beam evaporating the cloud and then a dry wind dissolving any leftover particles. This visualization took about three minutes. Part of me was afraid it wouldn't work, and another part of me was afraid of the implications if it did work. Sure enough, the cloud disappeared. It appeared that the structured energy of the thought form reorganized the cloud to be in harmony with the thought pattern.

Once we understand that our thoughts influence our physical reality, then we can become involved in the process of monitoring, changing, or fine-tuning them. This is the point where clear quartz crystal can enhance this process.

We shall now explore the second key to understanding the nature of reality as an energy system. *Everything in nature, includ-*

ing the human body, has an energy field. Our bodies do not stop with our physical form. We are essentially a *field* of energies which vibrate at different frequencies. Our physical body is surrounded by finer, more subtle frequencies of energy called the *aura.*

The aura can be sensed in various ways, and can be read as a "printout" of our thoughts. This printout can be visually perceived as changing colors or intuitively sensed as areas of even or uneven flows of energy. We refer to uneven flows of energy as *holes* or *dense spots.* By examining our auric fields at any given time, we can determine the nature of our thoughts and feelings, as well as their effects on our physical bodies. It is important to realize that *change begins with our thoughts.* We can creatively experiment with changing our thoughts and monitoring our progress by checking our energy fields. Symptoms and illnesses in our physical bodies, as they mirror the results of our thoughts, also serve as excellent biofeedback devices for learning about our thought patterns and belief systems.

A third basic concept upon which crystal healing and other healing systems are based is that *we can ultimately affect the health of our physical bodies, as well as our emotional, mental and spiritual states, by changing the energy field surrounding the body.* In our work we use healing thoughts, our understanding of energy, and various other tools to balance the energy field. During a healing session the auric field becomes clearer and the holes and dense spots even out. This creates an ideal environment in which to move toward change, growth, and optimal health. The key here is our free will. If we so choose, we can use our free will to block any changes in our energy field. On the other hand, if we choose to align our will and thoughts with a balanced energy field, it becomes easier to move into new levels of well-being and spiritual expansion. *Thoughts influence energy, and energy influences thought.* By changing our thoughts we can change our energy fields, and by changing and balancing our energy fields we can alter our thoughts.

NON-PHYSICAL OR SPIRITUAL PROPERTIES OF QUARTZ CRYSTAL

We have seen examples of how clear quartz crystal can amplify, transmit, focus, transform, and store electricity and sound energy in technology. Clear quartz crystal can also perform these very same functions with our thought and feeling energy.

Clear quartz crystal *amplifies* our intuitive, right-brain thoughts and perceptions, helping to increase our awareness of our intuitive language. I have learned about my own dominant modes of intuitive sensing through working with crystals. I tend to intuit through my feelings and internal sense perceptions, such as a sense of open energy flow, or a painful sense of pressure. You may personally discover a more vivid sense of color, a more detailed sense of imagery, and an increased awareness of sound. You may also experience a heightened sense of the energy flow in the body or refined tactile and kinesthetic sensations. You may even notice a greater sensitivity to receiving subtle mental impressions.

Clear quartz crystal *transmits* the healing qualities of life force energy and the light spectrum throughout our energy system. The healing qualities of color are just beginning to be rediscovered. The clarity of crystal makes it an ideal transmitter and amplifier of color in healing work.

The practice of *focusing* thought and receiving energy through a crystal for healing purposes is discussed in greater detail in Chapter 5 on programming crystals.

Clear quartz crystals are a balanced form of energy which has the ability to help *transform* an imbalanced field. It seems that the tendency of energy is to move from imbalance to balance, or from disorder to order. Therefore, when a more balanced field of energy (like a crystal) comes in contact with a less balanced field of energy (like a stressed-out you), your energy system will move toward balance and you will feel more energized.

Clear quartz crystal also has a unique ability to *store* thought forms which can be retrieved at a later time through meditation. The same highly ordered structure that has "room" for electrical sound and light frequencies also has room for thought frequencies. When you program a crystal you may notice that its energy changes. This ability to maintain a new level of energy is due to the crystal's modified internal structure.

Clear quartz crystal shares its gift of *communication* by acting as both a transformer and a catalyst in helping us to perceive other levels of reality and to understand our total spiritual nature.

A HISTORICAL PERSPECTIVE

We are now only beginning to understand what the ancients knew centuries ago: crystals play an important role in the evolution of society and human consciousness. Seeking spiritual understanding through religious practices has been an integral part of society in most cultures, including Western civilization, up until about four hundred years ago. The spiritual and physical aspects of nature were studied as one unit. The study of the stars included both what we call astronomy and astrology. Pythagoras developed mathematical principles which we still use today, as well as the principles which are basic to numerology, the sacred science of numbers. For Pythagoras, numbers had spiritual and physical properties. We are now becoming reacquainted with this idea as we study pyramid energies. Spiritual understanding of the universal laws comes to us through right-brain intuitive functions. It is interesting to note the lack of value placed upon the intuitive mode of knowledge in modern Western civilization.

In tribal cultures the shamans, or medicine men and women, served as doctors, teachers, and spiritual leaders. They were responsible for the health of the tribe at all levels. Shamans of every culture have used quartz crystal as a sacred power object in their medicine bags.

In ancient China, Taoist priests guarded the caverns where

crystals were found. The crystal caves were associated with sacred mountains having mystical properties, and were used in initiation rites. Disciples were led to a special stone bed were they were given a dream by the guardian spirit of the cave. Also, both the Japanese and Chinese have used crystal balls for contemplation for centuries.[1] Clear quartz crystal has been held in wide respect by many diverse peoples over many years.

There has been a variety of information channeled or intuitively received about the Atlantean civilization which began 50,000 years ago and allegedly sank about 12,000 B.C. The channelings described the integral part that crystals played in the technology and health of the Atlantean civilization. In her article, "Counseling with Crystals," Judith Larkin, Ph.D, described some ways crystals were used, as revealed through past life regressions:

"Crystals were used throughout Atlantean society. They were used as a central energy source for cities. A large crystal ball, thirty feet in diameter or larger, was located (some say suspended) under a pyramid-shaped roof. When meditated upon by specially trained persons, the crystal ball radiated energy much like a central electricity or nuclear energy plant, to power the entire city. The energy was absorbed outside the pyramid room by disc-shaped saucers and directed to specific areas of the town. Power crystals for large cities were immense, sometimes one or two miles in length. Crystals of this large size were not spherically shaped, but were housed under pyramid or dome-shaped roofs.

"In addition to the power crystal, there was a master crystal for each city or territory programmed to protect the area due to negative shifts in the planetary energy fields from astrological and social influences. With the use of this balancing master crystal, potential outbreaks of violence could be counteracted. For example, the often disturbing energies of the full moon could be calmed. Possible volcanic eruptions could be stabilized. The balancing master crystal bathed inhabitants in a soothing flow of energies conducive to human well-being, peace, and a sense of security.

"In addition to being sources of power and balancers of social energy, crystals were also used in Atlantean libraries. The libraries, rather than containing books, had their records imprinted in crystal plates or discs. The crystal plates carried a particular energy or vibration that children and students were taught to interpret psychically much the way Native American Indian tribes listened to the rocks talk and tell them stories of the planet's history and human events. . . .

"Communication in general in Atlantean times were nondiscursive and psychic in nature. Crystals were used in schools to teach children how to focus, amplify and transmit their thoughts without the need for vocalization. . . .

"Students were also taught through the use of the crystal how to focus and intensify their energy fields enough to vibrate them faster than the speed of light and to thereby dissolve, dematerialize, and, through thought projection, relocate their bodies, much like the 'Scotty, beam me up' dissolution of the physical body shown in *Star Trek*. Such 'beaming' was the major mode of transportation in Atlantean times. . . ."[2]

It is generally agreed that the misuse of quartz crystal by those greedy for power ultimately led to the destruction of the Atlantean civilization. "One abuse of the crystal was the implantation of small crystal rectangles in the base of the skull of servants, which were programmed so they would follow their masters' wishes."[3]

Another abuse involved battles for supremacy where specially constructed crystals were placed underground and activated with the sun in a special process. The energy was directed to destroy the temples, simulating earthquake activity.[4]

It has been said that some of the Atlanteans escaped to Egypt, preserving some of their knowledge in the Egyptian teachings. The Great Pyramid at Giza may have been a replica of the great temples of Atlantis. The big stones may have been cut by crystal lasers, and the pyramids constructed by using crystal power to levitate the stones. There are psychics who think that much of the ancient knowledge is stored in the pyramids and will be uncovered when we are ready to assimilate the information.

In addition to the pyramids, another unique and beautiful legacy, the *crystal skull*, reminds us of how much we have to learn about crystals. There have been several skulls found, and the most perfect skull was discovered in 1924 by Anna Mitchell Hedges in a Mayan temple in British Honduras. This skull is made from clear quartz crystal lacking any markings to indicate that it was carved. It has light pipes, prisms, and lenses within its eye sockets. Scientists are unable to date it, but the skull is considered to be between 20,000 and 500,000 years old. Psychics think it is a memory bank waiting to be decoded.[5]

With the current knowledge and understanding made available about clear quartz crystals, perhaps we now have the opportunity to once again expand our technology, and more importantly our spiritual wisdom, to bring a new level of peace and well-being to our planet.

SHAPES OF NATURAL CLEAR QUARTZ CRYSTAL

Single-pointed, clear quartz crystal is usually six-sided, with a flat base. Opposite sides are parallel. The base is often cloudy. Energy flows from the base to the point, or *termination*. The main energy transmissions come from the termination, so it helps if the termination and *pyramidal facets* are clear and perfect. From now on we will use the common term "point" to refer to the termination.

Sometimes crystals will have mineral inclusions, some of which are known as *phantoms*. They may also contain internal water or fractures that produce rainbows.

Small, clear points are among the most readily available and least expensive forms of crystals. We use them for meditation and healing.

FIGURE 1–1. Single-pointed clear quartz crystal.

Clusters are single points sharing a common quartz base. Their energy is more diffuse, and they can be used in a variety of ways to create a healing field in a room or on the body. Clusters are also readily available.

FIGURE 1–2. Clear quartz crystal clusters.

Double-terminated crystals are pointed at both ends. Energy flows in two directions like a battery, so these crystals are complete in themselves. Double-terminated crystals are useful in meditation on the third eye or on the crown of the head, and are good for programming. They are also good crystals to place on the body in healing. Unfortunately, they are among the most expensive and least available forms of crystal.

FIGURE 1–3. Double-terminated quartz crystal.

Rock crystal gives a more diffuse energy. It is often cut into different shapes such as balls and pyramids, and can be useful in meditation.

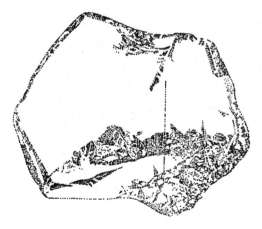

FIGURE 1–4. Rock crystal.

Lead crystal is a special kind of man-made leaded glass which does *not* have the specific properties of natural clear quartz crystal.

FIGURE 1–5. Lead crystal.

HOW QUARTZ CRYSTAL IS FORMED

Natural quartz is silicon diozide (SiO_2). It has a hexagonal crystal structure and a hardness of 7 on the Mohs' scale. (Diamond, the hardest mineral, has an index of 10.) The earth's crust is roughly 79% oxygen and silicon, in various silicate forms. Water is capable of dissolving silicon at about 600 degrees centigrade when under tons of compression. The process is similar to how rock candy crystals are made in a solution of sugar and hot water. The silicon dioxide passes up from deep within the earth and settles in different host rocks such as granite and sandstone. In most cases, the host rock is also some form of silicate. When silicon dioxide solidifies it bonds with the host silicate, and the crystals grow from the base into their hexagonal shape. If the host rock is not a silicate, such as dolomite, which is a form of calcium magnesium carbonate, then the liquid silicon dioxide does not bond with it. Instead, it crystallizes in all directions, forming double-terminated crystals.[6] Once out of the ground, crystals can be cleaned of surface minerals with oxalic acid.

Points and clusters are mined on a large scale in Arkansas and

Brazil, and fine specimens have been found in the Alps, the Pyrenees, and Madagascar. Brazil is also well known for its large supply of clear rock crystal.

THE CRYSTAL BRIDGE

A basic key to understanding man's relationship with nature is the awareness that everything in physical form is a gross manifestation of a subtle and infinitely more beautiful pattern existing in other dimensions. Clear quartz crystal can be seen as a physical manifestation of White Light. Because of its clarity the crystal has the capacity to receive and transmit a broad range of frequencies. As we learn to understand and merge with this member of Nature's Kingdom, we are led to a greater understanding of its patterns at other levels. The crystal then becomes a bridge to higher wisdom and expanded consciousness.

"Everything on planet Earth exists as an aspect of Universal Life Force Energy. You create changing patterns or forms of this energy as you interact with other members of your species and other Kingdoms of Nature. Energy is in a constant state of change. As you come into contact with Higher Light Beings or expand your consciousness through attunement with the Kingdoms of Nature, your vibratory rate changes. Your energy fields receive an influx of light from these sources that expands your sensitivity to the Higher Self, and to the God Consciousness that is present within all life forms. Your personal reality is a product of your beliefs, thoughts, and attitudes about life in general and about yourself in particular. You have free will to determine how open you are going to be to the Higher Light emanations that seek entrance into your fields of energy to facilitate an elevation in the state of your very Soul Essence."

2 | Choosing and Caring For Quartz Crystal

CHOOSING YOUR CRYSTAL

Choosing a crystal is a very personal process. Every crystal, as well as every human being, has its own unique energy field. Some crystals will feel more "energized" than others. In the same way, one crystal will evoke different responses from various people. For this reason, it is important to *affirm your own intuition* when choosing a crystal. People report feeling "drawn" to the same crystal repeatedly, or that one crystal seems to "speak" to them in some way. Try running your hand above a group of crystals, or hold them and see which ones you enjoy feeling. Trust your sensing and affirm that you are being drawn to the right crystals for you at this time.

In general, look for clarity, especially at the point and the pyramid facets. The points should be as perfect as possible. Any imperfections can diminish the effectiveness of the crystal, and alter the nature of the interaction between the crystal structure and life force energy.

Currently you can find crystals and crystal jewelry that have been symmetrically cut and polished. The use of these crystals is entirely a matter of your beliefs and personal preferences. It is important to work with what attracts you. All other considerations being equal, a large crystal will have more power.

Consider the purposes for your crystals. Smaller ones can be very effective as programmed crystals for meditation, while larger ones can be useful in balancing energies in healing. Crystals are like people—be sensitive and open to the unique gift each has to offer.

STORING YOUR CRYSTALS

Crystals like to be stored in sunlight and open spaces. They like to be used and enjoyed. Personal crystals can be kept in open, natural containers. Crystals whose purpose is to amplify the energies of an area love to be kept in sunlight. If you want to protect a crystal when carrying it, use natural fabric such as silk or cotton and make sure that the point is protected. You can use black, red, or violet material, or any other color that feels right to you.

If you store a crystal in the dark for a long period of time, it will need to be recharged in sunlight for optimal functioning.

CLEANING YOUR CRYSTALS

Over a period of time, quartz crystals can collect various forms of negative or static energies such as electronic pollution, negative thought forms and emotions, and loud and inharmonious sounds, as well as imbalanced electromagnetic energies. These imbalanced energies are picked up on the external surface of the crystal, and can affect the emanation of positive vibratory energy. Be aware of the fact that as a crystal balances particularly strong imbalanced energies, it may crack or develop inclusions. It is important to clean and charge a crystal when you first obtain it, and frequently thereafter, to keep it at its highest level of functioning.

Some symptoms of a crystal that needs to be cleaned are a sense of decreased energy coming from it, increased cloudiness within it, or stickiness to the touch. There are many ways to clean a crystal, so choose the method that seems right for you.

1. For *quick cleaning* after healing work or at the end of the day, hold the crystal under cold running water, pointing down, for half a minute or more. You should hold the crystal between both hands. Visualize white light clearing and illuminating the crystal. Thank and love the crystal for its service.

2. *Burn dried sage leaves* in a piece of pottery or abalone shell. You can buy sage leaves at an herb or health food store. Pass the crystal point up through the fragrant smoke, affirming that the crystal is pure and clear. Again, thank and love the crystal. Crystals can be soaked in sage tea. Sage has the ability to both clear and uplift the emotional, mental, and spiritual states, which is one reason why it was used by Native Americans as a purifier at the beginning of spiritual ceremonies.

3. Use your *breath to clear the crystal*. When you breathe you inhale and exhale life force energy. For this reason, the breath is a powerful tool for healing. Hold the crystal with your index finger on the largest pyramidal facet and inhale slowly and deeply. Now, hold your breath while you visualize and affirm the imbalanced energies being transformed and the crystal clearing. (Hold your breath only long enough to focus your thoughts. This is not intended to be an uncomfortable process.) Continue this thought visualization process while you exhale slowly through your nostrils onto the crystal. You will need to do this several times until the crystal feels like it has been cleared. Using the breath with crystal has been developed most thoroughly by Marcel Vogel, a former IBM senior research scientist currently doing crystal research.

4. For a more thorough cleaning, we like to place the crystals in a saltwater solution overnight or longer. We have used anywhere from one teaspoon to two tablespoons of sea salt per two cups of spring water, purchased from the grocery store.

5. Crystals can also be buried in sea salt for one to seven days. Sea salt attracts imbalanced energies like a magnet. However, the salt loses its strength as it neutralizes these energies, so the salt water or the sea salt must be thrown away periodically.

6. Crystals can be placed in the rain with the affirmation that they are being cleared.

7. If a crystal is carrying a particularly strong negative influence, it can buried under the earth for several days. It is a good idea to ask the Devas of the crystal and the earth to help you transform the imbalanced energy so that it doesn't remain in the earth in that state.

Take time to check your crystals often to see if they need cleaning.

CHARGING YOUR CRYSTALS

Once crystals have been cleaned and cleared of static, they must be charged with positive energies.

1. Quick charging is possible using the breath. Hold the crystal with the index finger on the pyramidal facet, as in the clearing exercise. Inhale slowly and deeply, hold your breath, and visualize the crystal charged with light, vitality, and love. Continue the visualization while you exhale through your nose in short bursts into the crystal. You will probably need to do this several times.

2. We like to charge crystals by placing them on a white cloth in direct sun for about six hours, and sometimes for a day and night in the full moon.

3. If for some reason six hours of sunlight is not possible, we ask the Devas and other spirits, who channel their healing energies through the crystals, to help charge and prepare them for healing use. We visualize the crystals as sparkling and clear and full of sunlight, and affirm that they are being fully charged.

4. We also charge crystals, particularly in inclement weather, by placing them on a crystal cluster or under a pyramid for a day or two. Pendants and other crystals that you carry with you can be washed and kept on a cluster or under a pyramid overnight, so that they are optimally charged for the next day. Our experience, however, is that they may eventually need to be cleared by other methods and recharged.

5. Crystals can be charged in snowstorms, thunderstorms, and and other dynamic weather conditions.

6. Keeping crystals in power spots, such as holy places or energy vortex fields, also charges them.

7. Crystals can be charged using the concentrated affirmation that they are filled with love and life force energy.

Crystals appreciate being treated with care and love. Be sensitive to their needs and they will reward you with expanding awareness.

3 | Exploring the Potential of Crystals

FAMILIARIZING YOURSELF WITH CRYSTALS

We will now give you some exercises to help you familiarize yourself with crystal energy. These ideas were drawn from several other sources[1] as well as from our own work. Exercise 3 introduces you to your *sensing hand,* the hand in which you feel sensations most strongly. In exercise 6 we introduce the terms *receiving* hand and *sending* hand, which relate to the magnetic polarities of your body. Further explanations of this concept are given in Chapters 6 and 8. We are introducing these terms now in order to help you determine the hand in which you will hold your crystal for healing work. Your sensing hand can be either your sending or receiving hand. We find that it varies from individual to individual.

Exercises

1. Take time to hold the crystal in the light and examine its beautiful facets. Let your imagination find the rainbows and galaxies in your crystal. Appreciate your crystal and thank it

for its unique gifts. Then close your eyes and remember as many details as possible about your crystal.

2. It is important to get a sense of how crystal energy feels. Hold your crystal in your left hand for a minute or so with the point toward your body. Be aware of any sensations or reactions. These are subtle sensations so if you don't feel anything at first, don't worry and just keep practicing. Also, notice where you feel reactions in your body. The energy seems to travel to where it is needed, so you may feel a tingling or warm sensation where the balancing is occurring. Now, try holding the crystal in your right hand and see if you notice any differences in the sensations you are receiving. Are the sensations stronger in one hand than in the other?

3. This exercise can help you find out which hand is your *sensing* hand. This is the hand which you use for sensing the energy in crystals or scanning the energy of another person's body. Your sensing hand is the hand in which you felt the sensations most strongly in the last exercise. Hold your hands about four inches apart as if you are holding an imaginary ball. Now hold the crystal in your right hand with the point facing toward the left palm. Draw circles in the field in front of your left palm. Be aware of the sensations. Repeat with the crystal in the left hand pointing toward the right palm. Your sensing hand will be the one in which the sensations are the most pronounced.

4. Hold the crystal in your left hand with the point toward your body for about thirty seconds. Then place it away from you for the same amount of time. Notice how you can feel the energy in your hand even when the crystal is not present. You may also notice energy building up in your hand or body. Be aware of any other changes.

5. Roll the crystal between your hands. Then hold it still in your left hand with the point toward your body. Repeat with your

right hand, and notice the *piezoelectric* effect, or the amplified strength of the crystal's energy.

6. To find out which are your *sending* and *receiving* hands you will need two crystals. In the healing model which we use, it is important to know which hand has a negative charge (receiving hand) and which hand has a positive charge (sending hand). Hold one crystal in your left hand with the point facing toward the body, and the other crystal in your right hand with the point facing away from your body. Sense the flow of energy in your body. Now, reverse the crystals so that the crystal in the left hand points out and the one in the right hand points in. Sense again. One circuit will probably feel more comfortable than the other. The hand where the crystal is pointing in becomes your receiving hand.

   If you don't have two crystals right now, another way you can check this is by using a pendulum (described in the next chapter). From now on we will use the terms "receiving" and "sending." If you are not sure, right-handers can use receiving to mean their left hand and sending to mean their right hand. Left-handers can do the reverse.

7. To get an idea of how it feels to work with the crystal on your third eye, hold the crystal in your right hand in front of your third eye with the point away from the forehead. Sense the energy. Now turn the crystal point toward your forehead and notice the difference. When you work with the crystal on your third eye, you will have to lay it on or tape it to your forehead, point up. Use hypoallergenic tape that you can purchase at the drugstore.

8. Now, hold the crystal point away from your third eye and imagine a color. Visualize the crystal as being this color. Concentrate on this image. Turn the crystal point toward your forehead and remain receptive. You can repeat this exercise using forms, images or feelings.

MEDITATION WITH QUARTZ CRYSTALS

Crystal is very beneficial for meditation. It can help you reach alpha and theta states more quickly and deeply because of its balancing effects. For this reason, simply holding a crystal can be very relaxing. The crystal also amplifies signals from your intuition, helping you to increase awareness of your own intuitive language. If you receive pictures or symbols, you may find them more vivid or prolific, similar to "tuning the picture" on a TV screen. If you receive "energy sensations" and feelings the subtle distinctions are more clearly perceived, making it easier to hear and sense your own wisdom.

The first step in working with the crystal is to attune it to your energies by holding it. There are several ways you can hold the crystal for meditation. One is to hold it in your receiving hand with the point toward the finger tips. If you wish to feel the concentrated energy from the crystal, the point can face toward you.

Another way to hold it is to cup your hands, placing your receiving hand on the bottom and your sending hand on the top. The crystal sits in your sending hand with the point upwards. It helps if the crystal has a flat base for this. You can also hold or tape the crystal to your third eye, point up. This position seems a little more sensitive than the others, so watch for dizziness, spaciness, or headaches. Our experience is that once you have adjusted to the increased amplification on your forehead, you will not experience these symptoms. Most of all, you should do what seems right at the time.

Crystals can help calm and focus any meditation practice: sitting, breathing, affirmations, visualizations, etc. You can keep a crystal cluster in your special meditation place to amplify higher energies. Breathing with the crystal helps you to attune to it.

The following simple meditation visualization can help you to relax and amplify your attunement with the Mother Earth:

While holding a crystal point up in your cupped hands, visualize yourself sitting in a favorite natural place. Im-

agine you are surrounded by a circle of crystals, points facing counterclockwise, with special ones pointing toward you at each of the four directions.

It may also be helpful to follow this visualization with a meditation for attuning with your crystal:

Become aware of how you are feeling physically, emotionally, mentally, and spiritually, as you prepare to sit with your meditation crystal . . . Take a few breaths, inhaling slowly, holding for a moment, then exhaling slowly . . . As you hold your crystal you may experience a variety of sensations such as temperature changes, tingling sensations, or a sense of expanding peace within yourself . . . It is good now to sit quietly in a receptive state, allowing the vibrations of the crystal to harmonize with yours . . . With thoughts of pure love and light ask your crystal to open an area of its structure so that you may enter inside its perfect form . . . Observe how your crystal creates a special space for you to come within its being . . . Enter your crystal now through the doorway of light provided for you . . . Feeling in a state of perfect balance, you choose to explore the interior of your crystal . . . Allow all of your senses to be open to experience your crystal . . . touch its sides, its foundations with your hands, your face . . . Allow your body to lean against a crystal wall . . . Listen for any sounds you may hear . . . Feel the sense of being at home, being totally welcomed by your crystal . . . Pause now in stillness for a few moments to allow the integration of the attunement . . . Prepare now to leave the crystal. Thank it for sharing its energies with you and return to the present.

It is important to be patient as you practice. Trust in your abilities to be at one with your Higher Self. Love yourself unconditionally, releasing fear and doubt. See yourself as crystal clear and filled with sparkling light.

OTHER SPECIAL USES FOR CRYSTALS

You can amplify your own body's energies by wearing or carrying a single-pointed or double-terminated crystal. The crystal helps stabilize and balance physical and emotional ups and downs, and helps transform any negative energies coming in. You can visualize yourself as "protected inside a large crystal and bathed in crystal light, with your energy focused upward through the point where it expands into the greater Light."

A pendant will stimulate and balance your energies in whatever direction the point is facing. Worn with the point down over the heart, it can ground your energies, stimulate your thymus gland, and amplify your sense of compassion. With the point up, your spiritual growth can be expanded. A double-terminated crystal accomplishes both tasks. A crystal worn at the throat will stimulate your thyroid gland and your creativity.

A pendant or crystal worn or carried on a daily basis needs to be cleaned often. You can hold it under running water, affirm its purity, and charge it overnight on a cluster. In our experience, however, more thorough cleanings are also necessary periodically.

A crystal can be placed under your pillow, point up, to help you remember your dreams. You may remember more details and the impressions may be more vivid. Double-terminated crystals are nice for this purpose, and you may be able to tape a small one to your third eye. In our experience, dream crystals may also need more frequent cleaning, because they do a lot of balancing while you sleep.

Quartz clusters love to be placed in a room where they are amplifying your loving vibrations and absorbing imbalanced energies. If you have been upset or had an argument, quickly clean and charge your clusters so they will be able to balance the imbalanced energy. Shirley MacLaine, in *Dancing in the Light*, says she puts clusters in the four corners of her bathtub as she takes a bath. If you do healing or body work you can put clusters around your room or under your healing table.

For increased growth and health of plants, place a crystal directly adjacent to the plant's stem, with the point upward. You can also keep clusters and other rocks around your plants because plants and rocks mutually benefit each other.

Through proper use, crystals teach us to honor all of nature, and to honor ourselves as co-creators of our universe. When we act clearly and with Love in our hearts, crystals can help us unite with the greater Truth and Light.

4 | The Crystal Pendulum: Contacting Higher Guidance

HOW TO USE THE CRYSTAL PENDULUM

Pendulums are an excellent tool for developing your intuition and self-awareness. Essentially, a crystal pendulum can be seen as a biofeedback device for monitoring attunement with your Higher Self. By listening to your Higher Self as you go about your daily life, you can also learn to fine-tune your discrimination in energy sensing.

Before using a pendulum, it helps to carry the crystal with you for a few days to attune it to your energy. When you are ready to begin, you can sit down at a table and hold the chain or cord of the pendulum with your thumb, index, and middle fingers. Your elbow should be resting comfortably on the table and your wrist straight. Experiment with the length of the chain or cord. A comfortable length will be approximately between three and twelve inches. In our experience the material of the chain or cord doesn't really matter.

It is very important to be relaxed and centered when using the pendulum. Take a few deep breaths, and visualize a place where you feel totally at peace. Affirm that your Higher Self is with you. Don't rush this relaxation. If you are not relaxed you will not get clear answers. In the beginning it is easy to become so worried about whether or not the pendulum will work that you can block the movement of the pendulum with your tension.

When you are ready, ask the pendulum to show you the movement for "yes" and the movement for "no." If you get no response, try holding the pendulum over the positive and then negative ends of a battery (not a dead one). You can use the movement over the positive end for "yes" and the movement over the negative end for "no." If this method does not work for you, don't despair. You can decide on a system such as clockwise (yes) and counterclockwise (no), or vertical (yes) and horizontal (no), or a combination of these positions.

Move the pendulum in your "yes" direction, visualizing YES in bold letters in your mind, and connecting to the sensation of the "yes" motion. Affirm that this is a "yes." Repeat with the "no" motion. Then ask your pendulum to show you a "yes" or a "no." This may take some practice over a period of time. It took me about two weeks to become comfortable with using the pendulum. Trust that you are learning and persevere until you get a response.

Now you are ready to begin asking questions that can be answered with a "yes" or a "no." When you are working with a pendulum, do *not* have your arms or legs crossed or touching each other. It is also good to wash your hands before starting. Work on an uncluttered surface, away from electrical equipment and magnets.

Ask your pendulum, "Are we in harmony?" or "Am I in tune with my pendulum?" *Readings are easily influenced by fatigue, illness, emotional states of mind, beliefs regarding the question, and any inharmonious energies which may be present.* Learning to stay in harmony with your pendulum is one of the most challenging lessons in working with it.

As you receive answers, listen to your "inner voice." Watch

for bodily sensations and inner perceptual sensations. We both get an uncomfortable pressure in our hands or an inner sensation of blocked energy when the answer is "no."

You are able to gain additional information by noting the strength of the pendulum's responses, particularly in healing work. In addition, you may being to receive responses from the pendulum different from your standard yes/no movement. At this time it would be a good idea to ask your pendulum to indicate how it would move for each of the following statements:

1. "Now is not the appropriate time to ask that question."

2. "I am not in tune with the pendulum."

3. "I need to clarify my question and ask it in a different way."

QUESTIONS TO ASK YOUR CRYSTAL PENDULUM

Now you are ready to use your pendulum in crystal work. Here are questions that can be answered with the pendulum. Ask them in a yes/no format. Some of these questions refer to ways of working with crystal that will be discussed in later chapters.

Choosing your crystal:

1. "Am I to work with you?" ("You" refers to a crystal.)

2. "Are you to be used in meditation/healing?"

Care of your crystal:

1. There are two ways you can find out whether a crystal needs to be cleaned. One is to hold the pendulum over the crystal

and ask the pendulum to show you its relative strength. If you get a "no," the crystal needs to be cleaned. Another way is to ask the crystal, "Do you need to be cleaned?"

2. Get a yes/no response for each of the following methods of cleaning crystals to find out how your crystal needs to be cleaned:

   a. Burying in sea salt

   b. Soaking in sea salt water

   c. Holding in sage smoke

   d. Breathing on it

   e. Putting crystal out in the rain

   f. Holding crystal under running water

   g. Burying crystal underground.

3. When you have had some practice with the pendulum, you can make an arc, and ask the pendulum to point to the optimal way to clean the particular crystal in the shortest period of time. Using an arc will save you time, as well.

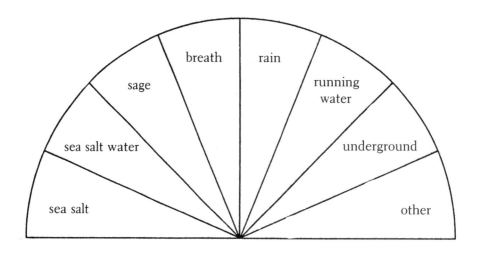

FIGURE 4–1. Pendulum arc for specific qualities.

4. "Should the crystal be cleaned for four hours, six hours, eight hours, overnight, twenty four hours?"

5. Recheck the crystal and ask, "Have you been adequately cleaned?" Sense the crystal with your hand. You can eventually learn by touch when the crystal is clean.

6. Ask: "How is the crystal to be charged?"
   a.   Affirmations
   b.   Breath
   c.   Sunlight
   d.   On a cluster
   e.   Under a pyramid
   f.   In a thunderstorm, etc.
   g.   For how long?

Uses for your crystal:

1. Location in a room: "Would you like to be on the window sill? By the bed? etc."

2. In meditation:
   a.   "Am I to sit with you in a totally receptive state?"
   b.   "Am I to actively access your memory for specific information?"
   c.   "Shall I place you in my receiving hand, on my heart, on my third eye?"

There are some other questions you can ask as you work with programming your crystals and using them for healing. These questions will be included in later chapters. However, you can already see the kind of clarification you can receive by using the pendulum.

Another kind of arc you can use with the pendulum is called the "confidence arc." This helps you to fine-tune the strength of a response.

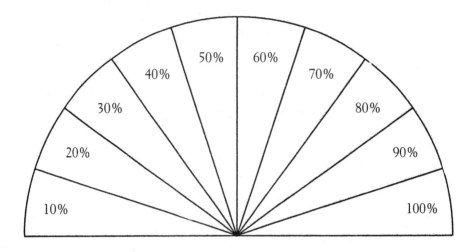

FIGURE 4–2. Confidence arc for pendulum.

For example, you can measure various crystals for use in meditation and to find out which one will be the strongest for you at this time. We have learned a great deal about our personal crystals through dialoguing with our pendulums.

DETERMINING YOUR SENDING AND RECEIVING HANDS

In a bar magnet the electromagnetic energies spin counterclockwise at the north pole and clockwise at the south pole.[1] If you hold a pendulum over the north pole and ask the pendulum to demonstrate the spin of energy at that pole, you will get a counterclockwise rotation. However, if you hold the pendulum over the north pole, *it will move in the direction of optimal balance* and rotate clockwise.

To determine your sending and receiving hands you can hold the pendulum over your left, then your right palm:

1. Ask your pendulum to show you the magnetic spin of your hand. If the rotation is clockwise, then that is your positive or sending hand.

2. Hold your pendulum over your palm and ask it to move in the direction of optimal balance. If it rotates clockwise, then that is your receiving hand, because the pendulum is moving in the opposite direction to balance the spin. If the rotation is counterclockwise, then that is your sending hand.

This is the procedure we use most often because in our belief system we ask the pendulum to move in the direction of optimal balance (or for the highest good). There is further discussion of the sending and receiving hands in Chapter 6, and of clockwise and counterclockwise rotation in Chapter 8.

You can use the crystal pendulum for *absentee healing,* using a picture or an image in your mind. You can infuse energy into a person (called the witness in radionics) by the following process. Begin sending healing energy to the person in your thoughts. The pendulum will probably start rotating to bring optimal balance. If the pendulum doesn't start to rotate you can initiate the motion. Continue sending energy until the pendulum becomes still. Then the session is complete.

There are many ways you can expand your work with the pendulum, and we hope we have stimulated your exploration in this area. The most important thing to remember is to remain centered and relaxed, learning to sense when you may be influencing the results. In this way you become more in harmony with your Higher Will.

5 | Programming Your Crystals

PROGRAMMING A CRYSTAL is a powerful way of co-creating for healing and transformation. A programmed crystal has the unique ability to amplify and continuously emanate programmed energy. One of my own more graphic experiences has been in working to remember my dreams. When I put a crystal under my pillow and affirmed that I would remember my dreams in the morning, I did indeed remember more of them. However, when I programmed the crystal to amplify my dreams so that I could recall them in the morning, the dreams were even more complete and vivid.

One way that a crystal becomes programmed with your intention is when you use it repeatedly for a specific purpose, such as meditation or healing. This is the simplest type of programming. When you want a crystal to retain a program over a period of time, it is more effective to program the crystal consciously. You can put more than one program into a crystal, but the programs need to be compatible. You should also wait a few days before adding another program so that the crystal can attune to the energy of the original program.

TYPES OF CRYSTALS TO BE PROGRAMMED

All crystals have a higher purpose to serve. Some crystals are better for meditation, and some for healing, and some are here as our "instructors." Such crystals already have data stored within them. Therefore, it is a good idea to ask your Higher Self, either through a crystal pendulum or through direct contact, whether or not there are any programs presently stored within your crystal. If there are, then you would work with it according to its highest purpose.

If a crystal has no previous programs, the next step is to use your pendulum to determine the most appropriate uses or programs.

PREPARING FOR PROGRAMMING

Spend some time with a pencil and paper writing a concise, potent affirmation that is for the "highest good of all concerned." You can ask your pendulum to help you to choose your wording: "Is this program worded appropriately for my highest good?"

STEPS FOR PROGRAMMING

There are many ways to program a crystal. Here are the steps we follow. Again, do what intuitively seems best for you.

1. Hold your crystal in your receiving hand. *Attune to the crystal*, sensing the energy coming from it, and visualize a bridge of pure white light connecting you with it. Say to your crystal, "I merge my being with you" (or thoughts to that effect), and sense your integration with it. Ask your pendulum, "Am I attuned to this crystal?"

2. Cup your sending hand inside your receiving hand, and place the crystal in your sending hand. *Ask your crystal to open a part of its matrix to receive the program.* It is important to ask permission of the crystal with honor and respect when programming, because you are essentially changing its structure. You can visualize an area of light opening up inside it. Wait receptively and allow your crystal half a minute or so to open. Ask with your pendulum, "Is your matrix adequately opened?" or "Are you prepared to receive the program?"

3. If you are programming color, sound, vibrations of a particular location, or other phenomena, you can put the crystal in the appropriate place and leave it for a period of time. If, for example, you are programming a piece of music into your crystal, ask your pendulum, "Shall I play this piece once, twice, etc., for it to be adequately programmed?" You will receive a yes/no answer. Or you can ask, after you have played the piece, "Are you adequately programmed with this music?" Then move to step six.

4. For a *thought* program you can *repeat your affirmation* three or more times, continuing your visualization and affirmation until you have a sense that you have done enough. Check with the pendulum, asking, "Is this crystal adequately programmed?"

5. Focus your awareness on your breath. *Breathe your affirmation* and love into the crystal in order to charge and attune with the new program.

6. *Affirm the protection* of pure white light around your crystal: "I surround you with the white light of love and protection." Thank the crystal for its service. You are affirming that this crystal, whose structure is altered with the addition of your program, will continue to serve the highest good of all concerned. Ask your pendulum, "Are you adequately protected?"

You are the only person who can remove a program that you have put into the crystal. *Cleaning and charging does not erase a program; conscious intent does.* To remove a program from a crystal, follow the same process you used to enter the program. Tell your crystal that you are focusing pure white light to erase the existing program.

As your life unfolds co-creatively with the mineral kingdom, keep in mind the qualities of trust and patience. Always honor the sacred space that is present within you as well as within the crystal. If you love and honor your crystal, it will respond in kind to you.

PROGRAMMING CRYSTALS FOR MEDITATION

When you work with meditation, you are usually operating in one of two modes. One mode is an active attempt to communicate with the Higher Self, and often involves a practice such as chanting a mantra or working with a visualization. A second, more receptive, mode involves silently observing or listening to your inner voice. A meditation crystal can be programmed to facilitate both modes, which is important because you often use both modes in one meditation sitting. With this crystal you can develop your own unique meditation program by adding a number of compatible programs, such as the following possibilities:

1. Music or sound that uplifts or centers you, such as a Beethoven symphony or the sound of a stream. Crystals work particularly well with amplifying the healing qualities of sound.

2. Work with specific affirmations such as:
    a. "I am relaxed, focused, and centered in Love."
    b. "I am merging with the Light."

3. Take this crystal to sacred places or energy vortex spots and program it to receive their energies.

4. Program specific power symbols from other cultures, such as the "Om" or "yin-yang" symbols, into the crystal by leaving the crystal on the symbol for a period of time.

A more specialized kind of meditation crystal would be one programmed with the *energies of a particular master teacher*. This is done by first merging your consciousness in the master and focusing your entire attention on the master as if the master were right there with you.

1. Read words that have been written by your master teacher to your crystal.

2. Repeatedly write his or her name on paper, while holding the crystal, then leave the crystal on the paper.

3. Work with pictures or photographs, leaving the crystal on them for a period of time.

4. Project or visualize the energy from a sacred place or object relating to the master teacher. Pure intent and pure love are essential in this process.

Another more specialized kind of crystal is the *Higher Self attunement crystal*. This crystal is more singularly focused on becoming more attuned to the Divine Will, and is used in the receptive mode.

1. For the initial program, work with a specific affirmation such as "My connection with my Higher Self is expanding and becoming clearer."

Many times you will find that the information received as you work receptively will clarify the initial program. Once the bridge to the Higher Self has been established, it is possible for different kinds of interdimensional communication to occur.

PROGRAMMING CRYSTALS FOR HEALING

In general, we program healing crystals "to not absorb imbalanced energy," especially if they will be held or used on the body. We find that crystals with this program need less frequent cleaning. This serves as a protection for the crystal and is a good program for crystals in daily use.

Here are some other suggestions for programs to use with healing crystals, particularly with ones you might place on the body.

Crystals for Physical Healing

1. "You surround me with Light and protection for my highest good" can be a good affirmation for a crystal that you wear or carry.

2. For healing a specific area of the body, you can visualize the area perfectly healed and project this image into the crystal, affirming your physical wholeness and perfection with love and confidence.

Crystals for Emotional/Mental Healing

In general, you can hold these crystals while working with specific issues, or you can wear them or carry them with you as you work with affirmations during the day. It is important to keep them cleaned and charged. These crystals can be protected with the programming phrase "without absorbing imbalanced energies." Here are some verbal and nonverbal ways you can program these crystals, as well as suggestions for specific healing purposes.

1. Use music that resonates with the affirmations you plan to use, and that represents for you the qualities of courage, patience, etc.

2. Affirmations for release:
   a. "You are a catalyst for bringing blocked energies into my conscious awareness for release."
   b. "You are a catalyst in helping me dialogue with my physical body without absorbing imbalanced energies."
   c. "You help me to open to forgiveness so I release the stored memories that block its flow."

3. Affirmations based on the colors:
   a. Red: "You help me move forward in life with courage and confidence."
   b. Orange: "You bring optimism and faith into my being."
   c. Yellow: "You bring joy, mental clarity, and confidence to all levels of my being."
   d. Green: "You bring emotional balance, harmony, and flow to all levels of my being."
   e. Blue: "My mind is steady, calm, and at peace."
   f. Indigo: "My inner sensitivity to all life is expanding and becoming clearer."
   g. Violet: "You are a catalyst to help me merge my personal will with the Divine Will, opening the way to the expansion of higher consciousness."

4. Crystals can be used to link directly with the subconscious mind where *past-life experiences* are stored. However, it is very important for your intentions to be pure before entering into this co-creative capacity with the crystal.

a. A good program would be: "You are accessing past life-times for lessons that can best be integrated at this time for my growth and highest good, without absorbing imbalanced energies."

b. A related program would be: "You are accessing past lifetimes that can become sources of strength, courage and further connection with my Higher Self in order to help me in this lifetime."

If you are guiding another person in a past life regression, it can be helpful to have two programmed crystals, one for each of you. This helps to deepen your attunement to the person being regressed.

5. Crystals can also be used to *see into the future*. (If you have apprehensions about this particular process then it is best not to explore it.)

An affirmation for seeing into the future could be: "Show me key elements that are ahead of me in this lifetime that I can now utilize, in order to truly achieve the highest purpose for my soul in this life." Also include a protection for this crystal.

OTHER TYPES OF PROGRAMS

Crystals have a powerful capacity for storing symbols, archetypes, and systems of thought. You can use this capacity to help deepen your knowledge of the symbol, etc. Follow the steps for programming and opening the matrix, then program the crystal to store and amplify the particular symbol information, placing the crystal on it.

1. For example, you can place a crystal on a *tarot* deck, or on a specific card, to help you deepen your understanding of particular cards and of the system itself.

2. In *astrology* you can use the crystal to better understand the symbolism and power of your key planetary configurations. The crystal would also amplify the positive effects of those configurations for your highest good. For example, if you want to understand and amplify the effects of a grand trine in your chart, write down the particular symbols that are involved, and draw the triangle on paper. Visualize and affirm that the energy of the configuration is assimilated within the structure of the crystal. You can also do this with *transits*, and later take the program out of the crystal once the transit has passed.

"Every crystal has a particular function in life and can gravitate to even greater levels of service and responsibility, through the influence of the conscious and subconscious energies emerging from the Human Kingdom. Whenever the crystal receives a visual imprint into its being, the picture is not only stored within, but is amplified geometrically each time that image is called for from the crystal in a meditation. Greater insights will emerge as you gain a greater awareness of the possibilities the crystal has to work with you."

PART TWO

Healing With Quartz Crystals

6 | The Human Energy System and the Crystal

COMPONENTS OF THE HUMAN ENERGY SYSTEM

In CHAPTER 1 we introduced the idea that there is an energy field surrounding our bodies. We call this energy field the *aura*, and it consists of patterned layers of energies vibrating at different frequencies. Everything in nature is surrounded by an aura, which serves as a template, or *blueprint, for the physical form.* In the 1960s Russian scientists Semyon and Valentina Kirlian sparked world interest by developing a technique to photograph these energy fields known as Kirlian photography. One of their most important findings is called the "phantom leaf" effect. After removing a portion of a plant leaf, they were able to photograph an energy field around the leaf as if the whole leaf were still present. They concluded that the energy field around the leaf forms a pattern which acts as an organizing force field for physical matter. The Russians referred to this "organizing field" as the *biological plasma body.* Einstein, in his unified field theory, also stressed that the energy field creates the form. If this is true, then

51

we should learn more about this energy field if we want to effectively heal ourselves on all levels. To do this we must first look at its "non-physical structure."

There is general agreement that the aura consists of a number of layers, or *subtle bodies*. However, perceptions vary as to the number of subtle bodies and their actual dimensions. Our particular working system roughly defines three layers of subtle bodies corresponding to the physical, emotional, mental, and spiritual levels of development. We combine the emotional and mental levels in our work, since they are both related to the fashioning of conscious beliefs.

The most physical layer is usually called the *etheric*, which seems to extend from about one-quarter inch to two or three inches from the gross physical body. It is sometimes seen as a thin band of white or grayish light, and, being the densest layer, it is the easiest to perceive. When we wear crystals or place them on the body, we are directly affecting the etheric body.

Surrounding the *etheric* body are the *emotional* and *mental* bodies. We are able to sense these layers from about three or four inches to about twelve inches from the body. These fields are often seen clairvoyantly as shimmering and changing colors that indicate the person's emotional and mental state.

From about twelve inches and extending at least another two or three feet from the physical body is the *spiritual* body. This is the level where we merge with our Higher Self and feel connected to the reality beyond our conscious everyday knowing.

Our subtle bodies are highly sensitive to thought forms. When a thought form enters one of our subtle bodies, the structure of that body changes to incorporate or resonate with the thought. Depending upon the nature of the thought, the subtle bodies either become more stablized, structured, and filled with life force energy, or the opposite process occurs and they become more disorganized. This process can happen instantaneously. For this reason, clairvoyants see many colors, some with more predominant overtones, and others more fleeting and changing. It is very important to understand that *we structure our very be-*

ings with our thoughts. It is also important to recognize that we can affect our sensitive energy fields in very positive ways to bring about balance and well-being.

In addition to serving as a blueprint for the body and as a record for our experiences, the layers or bodies of the aura also serve as *transducers of life force energy.* We receive life force energy from a variety of sources, including thought. These finer energies are stepped-down and made more dense at each level, until they assume a form that our bodies can use.

Another component of the human energy system is the *chakras.* The word "chakra" comes from the Sanskrit meaning "wheels of light," which is what they look like when photographed with Kirlian photography. "The Tibetans refer to these energy centers as 'khor-lo,' which also means wheel. . . . In the Bible, John refers to these energy centers as the 'seven seals on the back of the book of life.' . . . The Kabbalists refer to these centers as 'the seven centers in the soul of man.' There is obviously an historical cross-cultural tradition among many of the major religions that validates the existence of these subtle energy centers."[1] "These interdimensional chakras can be thought of, metaphorically, as tubes between the subtle bodies. When all subtle bodies are aligned, then all seven interdimensional chakra 'tubes' become synchronized, and cosmic energy flows through the body with the least resistance."[2]

A final component of our human energy system is the network of *nadis* and *meridians.* The nadis, described in Yoga and Ayurveda, are like spokes of a wheel radiating outward from each chakra, carrying transduced energy into the endocrine system and vital organs. The traditional system of Chinese medicine is based on stimulating the flow of *chi* through the meridians. These meridians are another system for transporting life force energy— much like a subtle nervous system. The texts of acupuncture describe twelve main organ meridians, eight "extraordinary vessels," and numerous sub-branches. It is possible that the acupuncture points of the Chinese system are the intersections of the nadis and the meridians.

What happens when we introduce crystal energy into the fields of the human energy system? In its natural state, the crystal's energy field is in a state of equilibrium. By definition, a balanced energy field has an abundance of life force energy. When the crystal's energy field has direct contact with our own, life force energy passes into the human energy system. It also follows that the more ways we find to incorporate clear quartz crystals, gemstones, herbs, natural foods, sunshine, fresh air, pets, houseplants, and other forms of nature into our lives, the more healthy and energized we will be.

THE HUMAN BODY AS A CRYSTAL

There are scientists who are interested in finding scientific explanations for how crystals work. Jonathan and I believe that we cannot fully understand crystal healing without exploring the non-physical or spiritual workings of reality. Nevertheless, the scientific view may offer some bridges to increase our understanding. One promising idea is the fact that the human body has properties similar to that of the crystal. In his book, *Spiritual Nutrition and the Rainbow Diet*, Gabriel Cousens, M.D., states:

> "The key of understanding the assimilation of energy into our physical structure is through the awareness of our bodies as a series of synchronous, interacting crystal structures. The human body on this level is a linkage of oscillating solid and liquid crystals that form an overall energy pattern for the total body. Each organ, gland, nerve system, cell, and protein structure—even the tissue salts of the body—are a level of organization with some degree of crystalline function."[3]

Human bone, as well as the supporting voluntary muscles and the arterial tissue in the cardiovascular system, are known to have piezoelectric properties. Bone demonstrates this property by generating a measurable electromagnetic field when stressed. It appears that bone also acts as an "antenna" for receiving information, and then transmitting it to the rest of the body via its crystalline properties.[4]

The ability of bone and quartz crystal to transmit energy demonstrates their capability as semi-conductors. Semi-conductors are substances whose conductivity is markedly improved by the application of heat, light, or electrical current. This phenomenon occurs only in substances having a highly ordered molecular structure, as in quartz crystal. In an ordered structure, electrons can move more easily from the electron cloud surrounding one atomic nucleus to the cloud surrounding another. The phenomenon of semi-conduction is also apparent in the human body:

> "Albert Szent-Gyorgi points out that the molecular structure of many parts of the cell is regular enough to support semi-conduction. . . . He conjectured that protein molecules, each having a slot or station for mobile electrons, could flow in a semi-conducting current over long distances without losing energy, much as in a game of checkers where one counter would jump along a row of other pieces across the entire board."[5]

Water is also a kind of semi-conductor. As a major component of the human body, it is capable of bringing ions into its structure and holding them in solution. This phenomenon is known as "structured water." When structured water in the blood organizes around an incoming micronutrient molecule, for example, it acts as a semi-conductor, moving ions into the structured cytoplasmic water of the cell. Optimally, ions and molecules with free-floating electrons, such as cell salts and other minerals, are attracted to the pattern created by structured water, establishing a resonance throughout the human body.

Therefore, in an imbalanced energy field there will be less

structure, thereby breaking down the semi-conducting properties of both water and protein. Cells are then not able to receive the ions they need.

We have given a scientific description of the crystalline properties of the human body. However, it seems that what we have said in scientific terms simply echoes these words from the Bible: "Man and woman are formed of the dust of the earth" (Genesis 2:7).

THE ELECTROMAGNETIC PROPERTIES OF LIFE FORCE ENERGY AND THE HUMAN BODY

In order to describe our model for healing, we must now introduce another property of life force energy and the human energy system. This property is their electromagnetic nature. "In 1861–62 Baron Karl von Reichenbach, a celebrated German chemist who discovered parafin, published a series of experiments on the *odic force*, or life force energy. His findings can be summarized as follows:

1. *Odyle* is a universal property of matter in variable and unequal distribution in both space and time.

2. It flows in concentrated form from special sources such as heat, friction, sound, electricity, light, lunar, solar and stellar rays, chemical action, and organic vital activity of living things.

3. *It possesses polarity.* There is both negative odyle, which gives a sensation of coolness and is pleasant, and positive odyle, which gives a sensation of warmth and discomfort.

4. It can be conducted: metals, glass, resin, silk, and water all being perfect conductors. . . . "[6]

Unfortunately, Baron von Reichenbach was largely ignored in his time, but current researchers are exploring some of his ideas, and demonstrating the *electromagnetic nature of the biological system*. Lakhovsky, in the *Secret Life of Plants*, states: "The cell-organic unit in all living beings, is nothing but an electromagnetic resonator, capable of emitting and absorbing radiation of a very high frequency. These fundamental principles cover the whole field of biology."[7]

More recently, Dr. Robert Becker, in his book *The Body Electric*, describes his research in the bio-electrical potential of cells, particularly bone cells, to regenerate and heal themselves with the addition of a weak electrical current.

Dr. Randolph Stone (1890–1981) founded a modern discipline of holistic healing, Polarity Therapy, based on a system of mapped magnetic polarities in the body. Dr. Stone, originally trained as an osteopath and chiropractor, developed this system after years of traveling and studying healing systems all over the world. He studied both yoga and Ayurvedic medicine in India and acupuncture and herbology in the Orient. He also learned concepts of healing with life force energy taught by Paracelsus, the sixteenth century prodigy sometimes considered to be the first modern medical scientist.

The general idea in polarity is that *if you connect a negatively charged body part with a positively charged body part, you stimulate life energy flow*. A positively charged area of the body correlates with the south magnetic pole, and a negatively charged area of the body correlates with the north magnetic pole. The healing system that we will describe later in the book uses the polarity of the body to stimulate a healing energy flow, so we will describe some relevant polarities.

The back of the head is considered positive, and the base of the spine is considered negative. In Dr. Stone's system the right hand and the right side of the body have a positive polarity, and the left hand and the left side have a negative polarity. However, we have not found this to be uniformly true. By holding a pendulum over a person's hand, or by asking the person to do the exercise in the section "Familiarizing yourself with crystals" in Chapter 3, we have found that for some people the right hand is negatively charged and the left hand is positively charged. This phenomenon seems somewhat related to whether a person is right- or left-handed, as well as to individual beliefs about how one gives or receives with one's hands. In our experience there has been no set pattern, and the charges have had to be individually determined. But in most cases, we have found that the right hand seems to be positively charged for right-handers, and the left hand positively charged for left-handers.

In our system of healing we use the mind to visualize the flow of life force energy going from the negatively charged hand (receiving hand) to the positively charged hand (sending hand), thereby creating a directional energy flow.

Many of you may have participated in a meditation or healing circle where you were asked to hold hands and visualize receiving white healing light through your left hand and sending it to the next person through your right hand. This visualization is an example of the same principle, using the hand polarity to stimulate energy flow. It has been our experience that for those whose receiving hand is not the left hand but the right, there may be less of a sensation of energy flow in this exercise. The point to remember here is that the body consists of negatively and positively charged areas, and that you can use your mind to direct life force energy from one area to another using magnetic principles of attraction.

We have seen how interconnected our energy system is. You can work with the meridians, the subtle bodies, or with your thoughts. We have chosen to work primarily with the chakras in the book because they are relatively easy to locate and there are many simple methods of balancing them with quartz crystals. Whatever method you choose will affect the whole system.

7 | The Chakras

W E HAVE DISCUSSED the connection of the chakras to the subtle bodies of the aura. Like the aura, the chakras can be said to be a "record" of our experiences. Every chakra, when balanced, reflects a particular pattern of energy that can be sensed as a different color or perceived as a "sense perception." Using an analogy, we might say that the chakras are like windows in a house—that "house" being our body. If the windows are small or dirty, or if we close the curtains, less light can come in. In this condition, bright sunlight outside might appear as a cloudy yellow color inside the house. The degree to which the chakras are activated, balanced and able to receive life force energy depends upon our will, our belief system, and our emotional state.

We have also discussed how the chakras work to *step-down* life force energy into a form which can be used by the physical body. The chakras stimulate the endocrine glands, which, in turn, secrete hormones for cell growth and maintenance as well as other bodily functions. If an endocrine gland does not receive sufficient life force energy, the system does not function properly and the result is pain, or *dis-ease*. Actually, pain and disease can be seen as a message that, in some way, thoughts are blocking the flow of life force energy.

When an imbalance is present in a particular chakra, the key to restoring harmony in the system lies in developing the characteristic qualities which that chakra represents. For example, if we find it difficult to express our needs, truth, or creativity, the result will be a restricted flow of energy in the throat chakra. To remedy this, we can sing. Singing can help balance the throat chakra and also uplift the spirit. By monitoring the energy flow in the chakras, we can receive accurate feedback on which of our beliefs promotes physical vitality, peace of mind, and strengthened intuitive awareness. These are the beliefs that will help connect us to the Source of all life.

ROOT CHAKRA

The root chakra has a strong affinity with our etheric body, which, in turn, is intimately connected with the gross physical body. The etheric body is linked to physical vitality, mastery of our physical bodies, and our survival sense in the physical world. When we are physically tired or stressed from physical exertion, the root chakra may feel like it needs to be charged or revitalized.

On the emotional and mental levels of our development, the root chakra expresses personal will and the desire to take action and to express ourselves in unique ways. If the root chakra is congested or deactivated, we may perceive the world as being threatening or unsafe, or we may not be able to express something that feels very basic to our individual nature.

On the spiritual level of development, the root chakra can be expressed by the following exclamation: "The universe resounds with the joyful cry, I AM" (Scriabin). This is like a baby's total and spontaneous joy and delight in being. If we have deep-rooted beliefs that we don't deserve to live, that there is no place for us in the universe, or that somehow we cannot find and appreciate our uniqueness, then this may deactivate the root chakra. "Like the trees and the stars, you have a right to be here" (Desiderata).

FIGURE 7–1. Diagram of chakras.

The color of the spectrum associated with the root chakra is *red,* which is an intense, focused vibration that builds vitality on the physical level and courage, perseverance, and strength on the emotional, mental, and spiritual levels.

1. Meaning: Physical vitality, basic will to be

2. Associated color: Red

3. Associated tone of the scale: C

4. Endocrine glands: Gonads or adrenals, depending on the belief systems associated with our basic being.

5. Affirmations:

   a. "I honor the natural physical vitality of my body and take care of it wisely."

   b. "I AM, and the world welcomes me."

   c. "I live courageously, taking action to express my being."

6. Location: Base of the spine, pubic bone.

LOWER ABDOMEN OR SPLEEN CHAKRA

In the traditional yogic system of chakras, the second chakra is located two or three inches below the navel. Some Western systems locate this chakra in the area of the spleen. In our experience, the energy of these two areas are definitely related, so we speak of them as one chakra. This chakra is particularly associated with the *etheric* and *emotional* subtle bodies. The first step in life is to establish our sense of being (physical/etheric level). Then we reach out and begin to connect with others and establish who we are on the feeling level of relationship (emotional level).

On the physical level of development, the lower abdomen

chakra deals with *assimilation* and *elimination* (letting go). This chakra also deals with an exploration of our physical senses and of sense pleasures in the physical world. Deactivation of this chakra generally stems from overgratification of the senses. Unbalanced eating, drinking, and sexual habits often develop out of our need for security and our inability to "let go." So at the physical level we must learn moderation.

On the emotional level of development, we begin to connect with others and to seek their approval in order to validate who we are. We assimilate the impressions that others have of us and seek to understand ourselves through these "mirrored" impressions.

Sometimes deactivation of this chakra is related to holding on to old grievances and refusing to assimilate new understandings. We prefer security to change because of our sense of being "incomplete." So we attempt to fill up our emptiness by trying to take in love in the form of pleasure.

On the spiritual level of development, the lower abdomen chakra relates to the joy of being alive and to understanding the connectedness of all life. If we are blocked at this level of development, we may feel loneliness or basic separateness.

Many of us at times experience deactivation in the lower abdomen chakra, because we are still learning to moderate our desires and to release our desire for security. Here we are working with our desire for approval and learning how to connect with others in ways that support our uniqueness.

The lower abdomen chakra is associated with the color *orange,* which is a warm, expansive vibration that transmits qualities of stimulation, optimism, hope, and sociability. Orange is a good color to help banish fear and depression, and to help us reach out to others and new adventures.

1. Meaning: Connecting with others through our feelings, assimilating and letting go of our experience.

2. Associated color: Orange

3. Associated tone of the scale: D

4. Endocrine glands: Spleen, liver, pancreas, gonads

5. Affirmations:

   a. "I assimilate right understanding through my feelings and senses.

   b. "I welcome change and freely let go of what I don't need.

   c. "I am enough."

   d. "I trust the universe to supply my abundance and prosperity."

6. Location: Two inches below navel (also, lower abdomenal area and spleen).

SOLAR PLEXUS CHAKRA

The solar plexus chakra is associated with our sense of personal identity and power and has an affinity with the emotional and mental subtle bodies. On the physical level, the solar plexus relates to learning how to both mobilize and regulate energy for conscious purposes. On the emotional and mental levels, we establish and develop who we are and learn to feel powerful in our uniqueness. Here the emphasis is on learning how to develop our self-esteem and to free ourselves from the roles we feel bound to play in life. When we are blocked at the emotional level, we may feel angry at having to work at a job that does not express who we are, or at filling others' needs without meeting our own. We may also be afraid to step forward and get what we need.

On the mental level of development, we learn to make conscious choices about what we want, and to expand who we are through new skills and information. So our task at the solar plexus is to consciously use our mind to choose and develop a positive self-image, construct our own set of values and establish a base of personal power.

If we are afraid to let in new ideas or hold onto old values, we may be blocked on the mental level of this chakra. If we lack confidence or a sense of power, we may sense a lack of energy here. We know that self doubts or the belief that we don't deserve the good things in life can give rise to "butterflies in the stomach." Often, in trying to deal with our emotions relating both to confidence and self-acceptance, we develop an imbalance in both the lower abdomen and solar plexus chakras. Repressed anger as well as an inability to express our personal power may deactivate both the root and solar plexus chakras.

On the spiritual level, the solar plexus chakra can be expressed as "I am unique and I walk my path with an unassuming self-assurance." This is like being in a garden and noticing the beauty of each and every flower. They are all beautiful and they are all distinct. Together, they express the manner in which diversity and uniqueness contribute to the beauty of the whole. Blockage at the spiritual level can manifest through lack of self-confidence as well as conflicts concerning whether it is "right" to believe in oneself. In the history of Christianity, and in other religious traditions, "selfishness" was considered to be a sin. Many of us still carry past-life memories from earlier Christian times and have a great deal of conflict about affirming ourselves. For us, one answer lies in observing the beauty and uniqueness of every living thing in nature.

The color associated with the solar plexus is *yellow*, a lighter, stimulating vibration with qualities of joy, optimism, and confidence. These are qualities we normally relate to the sun. Yellow also has the quality of helping to focus and expand the conscious, decision-making mind.

1. Meaning: Developing self-confidence and building personal power

2. Associated color: Yellow

3. Associated tone on the scale: E

4. Endocrine glands: Adrenals, liver, pancreas

5. Affirmations:

   a. "I own my strength and power."

   b. "I appreciate all my wonderful qualities that make me unique."

6. Location: Two inches above the navel.

HEART CHAKRA

The heart chakra has an affinity with the emotional, mental, and spiritual subtle bodies. Here we learn about compassion for ourselves and others, and we experience the truth of the Oneness of all creation. On the physical level, the heart chakra relates to our physical hearts as well as to blood circulation. The thymus gland, which is also located in this region, has a strong influence on our immune system.

On the emotional and mental levels of development, we must learn the importance of self-acceptance, forgiveness, and a non-judgmental attitude towards ourselves and others. Many of those who suffer heart attacks are perfectionists who may harbor anger and judgment for the mistakes of others. Lack of compassion and an overly judgmental attitude can deactivate the heart chakra, as well as the lower abdomen and solar plexus. We must learn to accept our emotions as part of our being. Our emotional responses, such as anger or fear, can often give us instant feedback on the direct consequences of our choices and decisions. Ultimately, this feedback helps us to move towards union with *God/Goddess/All That is*, rather than continuing to exist in a state of separateness.

On the spiritual level, the heart chakra is associated with the understanding that we are all One—that we are connected rather than being separate from others. When someone has died or left us and we feel separate or lonely, we may deactivate the heart chakra if we try to repress the grief and sorrow. In general, we can lose energy at our heart chakra, and the lower abdomen chakra as well, if we repress our feelings due to our belief that "it is weak to express feelings." Often forgiveness needs to occur at the heart, particularly self-forgiveness.

The color *green* is associated with the heart and it is a soothing, balancing vibration associated with harmony and compassion. I've often thought that the reason that we are surrounded by so much green in nature is to teach us about balance and compassion.

1. Meaning: Developing compassion for all, especially ourselves

2. Associated color: Green

3. Associated tone of the scale: F

4. Endocrine gland: Thymus

5. Affirmations:
   a. "I accept myself fully as I am."
   b. "I am truly loved."

6. Location: Heart.

THROAT CHAKRA

The throat chakra has an affinity with the emotional, mental, and spiritual bodies, particularly the latter two. It is related to the solar plexus chakra, as both areas deal with self-expression. Emphasis at the throat is on expressing our truth and creativity and giving service to others. On the physical and emotional levels, fear of expressing something that needs to be said may create blockages resulting in sore throats and other throat problems.

On the mental level the throat chakra relates to our ability to give to others through our creativity, and the active expression of our knowledge. If we do not believe that we have something to give, or if our creative expression has been blocked, we may lose energy at the throat. Many of us have had experiences in school in which our creative expression was severely limited. Consequently, we are now learning to activate our throat chakras.

At the spiritual level of development, the throat chakra relates to service. We learn that giving to others through our uniqueness is our major function in being on the earth. It has been said that the throat chakra relates to the will. I believe that our lesson at the throat chakra is to put our will into action through service, and to make that service a creative expression of our individuality.

The color *blue* associated with the throat chakra brings mental peace and understanding. As blue is the color of the sky, it is also an expression of our aspirations.

1. Meaning: Speaking our truth, creative expression, giving service

2. Associated color: Blue

3. Associated tone of the scale: G

4. Endocrine gland: Thyroid

5. Affirmations:
    a. "I now say what needs to be said."
    b. "I value and express my creativity."
    c. "My purpose is to serve others with my unique gifts."

6. Location: Throat.

THIRD EYE CHAKRA

While the third eye chakra is associated primarily with the spiritual subtle body, it serves a unique role as a *coordinator and regulator at the physical, emotional, and mental levels of development.* This chakra and the lower abdominal chakra have a complementary relationship, both focusing on our connection with life and on the processes of assimilation and elimination. On the physical level of development at the third eye chakra, the pituitary, or master gland, has a regulating function in the body. We can think of the third eye as a supervisor of our affairs, with the solar plexus often acting as the foreman, and the organs actually carrying out the orders.

On the emotional and mental levels of development, we consciously and unconsciously choose the beliefs which determine our reality. *The third eye chakra enables our beliefs to be manifested.* Our subconscious mind is located here, and often our subconscious memories from childhood or past lives deactivate the third eye chakra. When we work with energy balancing, we usually put a crystal or gemstone on the third eye in order to affect the overall system. Sometimes the root of the change needs to begin here.

On the spiritual level of development, the third eye serves as a catalyst or bridge to help us connect with our higher spiritual nature. It is the seat of our intuition. As we contact and merge with the awareness of unity, we begin to receive additional impressions from beyond our five senses and everyday mind. Intuition feels like a calm sense of rightness, even when it appears in the midst of pain. Intuitive knowing comes in many forms, such as dreams, colors, symbols, sounds, pictures, feelings, sense impressions, and, quite frequently, as an ordinary thought. We can block our intuition and deactivate our third eye chakra through fear of the unknown, or our belief that knowledge can only be obtained through the rational mind and physical senses.

The color associated with the third eye is *indigo*, which is a deep blue tinged with violet, like the color of the twilight sky. Indigo is a very light, cooling, uplifting vibration which has the quality of expanding spiritual understanding.

1. Meaning: Regulator and catalyst, seat of our intuitive knowing

2. Associated color: Indigo

3. Associated tone of the scale: A

4. Endocrine gland: Pituitary

5. Affirmations:
   a. "I now release early life and past life experiences which do not serve my highest good."
   b. "I accept responsibility for creating my reality."
   c. "My intuitive connection with my higher spiritual nature is expanding and becoming clearer."

6. Location: Brow.

CROWN CHAKRA

The crown chakra has an affinity with our spiritual subtle body. This chakra and the root chakra share a common focus on our basic sense of identity. However, at the crown we do not emphasize our individual uniqueness. Here our emphasis is on our universality, on merging with the Oneness of All Things. The crown is where we become One again, and merge with a sense of Infinite Peace and Joy—the Unity of All Life. *An imbalance at the crown chakra often means that at that moment we do not wish to receive guidance from our Higher Self.* We are holding on to some belief because it is familiar, even if it is painful. Often, moving to a new level of integration involves the death of some part of us. There are times when we hold on from fear of the unknown and block the love and safety that flows into us at the crown chakra.

The color associated with the crown chakra is *violet*. It has a vibration that gives rise to alpha and theta brain waves. Violet also promotes the qualities of transformation and transcendence.

1. Meaning: Merging with our basic identity of God/Goddess/All That Is

2. Associated color: Violet

3. Associated tone of the scale: B

4. Endocrine gland: Pineal

5. Affirmations:

   a. "I merge with the Unity of All Life."

   b. "I act in alignment with my Higher Spiritual Nature."

6. Location: Crown of the head.

RELATIONSHIPS OF THE CHAKRAS

When you sense imbalances in particular chakras, you can use your understanding of their nature and function to help clear negative beliefs. You can also look for a connection between deactivated chakras. For example, if the root, heart and throat chakras are deactivated, you can be fairly certain that something is not being expressed or communicated. In general, the quality of the energy received at the three upper chakras—the throat, brow, and crown—depends on the quality of energy at the three lower chakras: the root, lower abdomen, and solar plexus. We can improve the quality of energy flow through the chakra system by focusing unconditional love and acceptance from our hearts on any deactivated chakra. In our practice we also check the complementary pairs of chakras because they often function together:

Root Chakra—Crown Chakra

Lower Abdomen Chakra—Third Eye Chakra

Solar Plexus Chakra—Throat Chakra

Heart Chakra

Sometimes we find that working with the most deactivated chakra will help to clear and balance the entire system. When you have finished working with the chakras, it is helpful to affirm total love and unconditional acceptance in your heart. During the clearing and affirmation process you can monitor the energy flow in the chakras, and in this way receive immediate feedback on what gives optimal balance.

8 | The Healing Process

THE THREE STEPS OF HEALING

Healing can be viewed as a three-step process. This involves *clearing* out the blocked energy that impedes growth, *infusing* positive healing energies, and *expanding spiritual awareness* through contacting the Higher Self.

As we have seen before, repeated negative thoughts disrupt or disorganize our energy fields, causing a restricted flow of life force energy. We often retain negative thoughts because of the subconscious belief that self-examination will only recreate the pain and perpetuate it indefinitely. This "package" of negative thoughts and feelings is then stored in our subconscious, in our subtle bodies, and in our physical body. This, in turn, manifests as an altered energy flow, making us feel "out of balance." If this blockage is not cleared, toxic wastes can build up, cells do not function optimally, and physical deterioration and disease can result.

The effects of negative thought patterns in the body can be essentially healed by reprogramming our subconscious with positive, life-affirming thought patterns. However, the ultimate healing solution is the act of loving and accepting oneself on the deepest level. It is possible to find the places inside ourselves that are hurting, and to give that part of us the compassion which can heal the pain. When we can establish our own confidence, inner peace, and self-acceptance, it is possible to forgive and accept ourselves, as well as others.

When you work with others it is important to hold their perfection firmly in your mind. You must see yourself as a channel for light, unconditional love, and eternal peace. This surrounds the person with the energy of compassion, which acts as a catalyst for him or her to heal a negative throught pattern.

The first step in this model of healing is *clearing*. This involves becoming aware of negative thoughts, clearing them through visualization, releasing the accompanying emotions, and finally clearing the energy field itself. This is an important step because it is the *mind that controls the energy flow*. A moment of awareness and loving release can clear the energy field, bringing a noticeable difference in how one feels.

Once the blockages are cleared, the second step is to *infuse* energy into specific areas, so that the electromagnetic field is balanced and energies are flowing evenly once again. This is done with positive, affirming thoughts and visualizations, and an attitude of compassion. An example of this infusion would be visualizing an area of the body in complete balance, affirming that we are healthy, loved, and filled with vital life force energy like rivers of light. Work is also done with the electromagnetic field to infuse energy in specific areas, balance each chakra, and move energies evenly through the field.

The third step, spiritual expansion, is *contacting and being receptive to the Higher Self* through visualization and attunement. Chakras can be expanded and the electromagnetic field energies heightened for increased spiritual awareness through the use of *crystal grids*, which we will discuss later in this chapter. We will also cover this third step of the crystal healing process in the Level I and Level II healing formats described in Chapter 10 and 11.

BALANCING YOUR BODY'S ENERGIES WITH CRYSTALS: CLEARING

Crystals can be helpful in all three stages of attitudinal healing, and there are a number of ways you can use them to balance your body's energy field. In the method we describe here, we use our minds to direct the energy flow, and work with the magnetic polarities of our hands. We like this method because it works well with the three-step process of clearing, infusing, and expansion.

The clearing process can work to relieve pain when the pain is a sign of blockage or disruption in the energy flow. We use this process to help relieve headaches, muscle cramps, congestion, and fever, as well as bottled-up fear, anger, and grief.

1. Place your receiving hand on or slightly off the painful area and get a sense of what the energy feels like. You may feel a lack of energy flow, pain, pressure, cold, heat, or "uncomfortableness" in your hand.

2. Hold the crystal in your sending hand, rotating it down by your side in a counterclockwise circle. Continue rotating until you feel some pain relief or get a sense of an energy flow returning to the area. This can take anywhere from one to ten minutes. Ask your pendulum, "Do I need to continue the clearing process?" By continuing to sense what is happening in your hands and using your pendulum for feedback, you will learn to know when the energy is flowing again.

Just working with the clearing process can yield useful and even dramatic results. Here is an example of a crystal healing incident related to us by a friend:

"My baby Alden had a fever and was listless and fussy. I received instructions on the phone from a friend who knew about crystals, and I held the crystal and my other hand the

Figure 8–1. Clearing energy.

way he suggested. I also visualized the sick energy leaving Alden's head, going into my fingertips and out through the crystal. When it seemed enough time, the crystal stopped as if an electric current had stopped. In about five minutes Alden woke up crying, and then he settled down. The fever was gone and it didn't return."

Another woman took our crystal class and was very enthusiastic about starting to use crystals. Her opportunity came several days later when she was teaching an art class. A student of hers had come with a terrible headache and wanted to leave class. She convinced the student to lie down for a few minutes with her own left hand on her forehead and with a crystal in her right hand pointing toward the finger tips. The student felt much better in about five minutes and returned to class dumbfounded that a crystal might have helped her in some way. Our friend was elated and has continued to use crystals in innovative ways ever since.

BALANCING YOUR BODY'S ENERGIES WITH CRYSTALS: INFUSING

After there is an even flow of energy from the clearing process, we usually infuse or add life force energy to continue the process of healing.

1. Hold your receiving hand palm up and visualize it receiving life force energy.

2. Hold the crystal in your sending hand, pointing toward your fingertips and toward your body. Rotate the crystal counterclockwise over an area of your body, visualizing life force energy coming through the crystal and into your body. Continue rotating until you get a sense in your receiving hand or in your body that the area has received enough energy. Ask

FIGURE 8-2. Infusing energy. Notice that the counterclockwise rotation is as though you are in front of your body, facing it.

your pendulum, "Have I infused enough energy into this area? "Again, this can take anywhere from one to five, or even ten, minutes, although in our experience it takes less time to infuse energy than it does to get energy flowing again by clearing.

Infusing energy can be particularly helpful for everyday stress and fatigue. It is also effective in building up energy in an area for long-term healing, and for creating new affirmative patterns of thought. In our experience, using the two steps together, first clearing and then infusing, brings the greatest benefit.

We visited a woman who had recently had abdominal surgery and was recuperating at home. She had been unable to breathe deeply and was too weak to get out of bed. We began with the clearing process, and the energy began to flow very quickly. We know that what she needed, however, was a strong infusion of energy. So we placed three crystals on the bed pointing toward her body. We worked with the infusing process for about five minutes or so. She began to breathe deeply, and we worked a little more, until we felt she had taken in all the energy she could assimilate at that time. She was then able to get up and walk a few steps.

She later wrote us, saying, "Thank you for your time and effort on my behalf. I truly believe that the crystals and you two cut my healing time from intestinal surgery in half."

Our personal belief is that *illness first begins with imbalanced thoughts accompanied by emotional pain.* We try to help people become more aware of the imbalanced thought and to release the accompanying emotional pain. Consequently, most of our work has been with counseling rather than direct work with physical ailments. However, release of thought imbalances can sometimes have an immediate and direct physical impact.

A client with a bladder infection came to us as a last resort. She had a doctor's appointment following our session. As we talked, she began to realize how angry ("pissed off") she was about not being able to express herself in a certain situation. We then had her lie on the healing table (fully clothed) and began to clear the bladder area, while we encouraged her to voice her anger. We then infused energy and completed the healing session. The subsequent doctor's examination showed no trace of infection.

Releasing painful past experiences and realigning our thinking takes effort and patience. Crystals can amplify the process but they are not an instant cure. They are a subtle tool which we can choose to use in our everyday life.

A practice you can try daily when you wake up in the morning (instead of reaching for the coffee) is a *chakra infusion*. You can also try this when you are feeling tired or unsettled. To do a chakra infusion, simply hold the crystal in your sending hand and rotate counterclockwise over each chakra, beginning with the root, for about a half a minute. Try to sense when the chakra has assimilated enough energy. Then hold the crystal steady, pointing toward the chakra and affirm, "I am now optimally balanced." Then move to the next chakra. Afterward you will feel more energized and more balanced emotionally. We feel a sense of evenness, peace, and well-being. Giving ourselves a chakra infusion morning and evening has helped conserve and regenerate our energy when we travel. I have also noticed that if I give myself a chakra infusion for two or three days preceding my menstral period, uncomfortable physical symptoms are relieved.

ANOTHER INFUSING POSITION

Another variation of the infusion process works with the same hand principles as shown in the illustration. Hold the crystal in your receiving hand with the point toward the body and hold your sending hand on or slightly off the area of the body on which you are working. If you have two crystals then you can also have a crystal in your sending hand with the point toward your fingertips. You will be increasing the life force energy flow to the

FIGURE 8-3. Another infusing position.

area as it moves from your negative receiving hand to your positive sending hand and into the body. This is a comfortable position in which to rest awhile, and the process will take longer than if the sending hand is actively rotating the crystal.

CLOCKWISE AND COUNTERCLOCKWISE ROTATION

Our hypothesis of why these methods work is that, first of all, an imbalanced area has an overabundance of positive ions. This may be because the free-floating electrons from the negative ions are unable to move in a disorganized field, as we discussed earlier. At any rate, we know that positive ions are associated with imbalanced energy, and that negative ion generators bring a sense of harmony. We also hypothesize that salt works as a cleanser for quartz crystal because it neutralizes the positive ions that have collected on the surface.

When you place your negatively charged hand over an imbalanced area during clearing, the attracted positive ions begin flowing through your body and out your sending hand. The flow of energy is expedited when you rotate counterclockwise (negative rotation) with your positively charged sending hand. If you rotate clockwise there is no sense of flow because the positive ions are not neutralized by your sending hand. Once the positive-negative balance is restored, we perceive an energy flow.

We have been asked, "Aren't you taking imbalanced energy into your body by this method?" The answer is that the energy flow going through your body is neutral in its effects unless you take in imbalanced energy through your thoughts. You can prevent this from occurring by remaining still and receptive in your mind and using only your hands. If this is not an issue, you can actively work with your mind and visualize an energy flow. Amplifying the energy flow with our thoughts works best for us.

In the infusing process you have more flexibility about

whether you wish to rotate counterclockwise or clockwise. *If you rotate clockwise (positive charge) with your sending hand (positive charge) the energy coming from the crystal in your sending hand is more intensely focused.* We use a clockwise rotation when we wish to infuse a specific energy such as a programmed crystal on the body. Our experience has been that clients feel a stronger sense of energy from a clockwise rotation.

If you rotate counterclockwise (negative charge) with the crystal in your sending hand (positive charge) the energy flow seems to cover a broader area. In our experience a counterclockwise rotation takes longer and creates a more gentle effect. Our guidance has been to use a counterclockwise rotation most of the time. However, we have used both rotations at the same time. This involves rotating the crystal clockwise first to *infuse* a particular energy in a focused manner, and then to *expand* the focus with a counterclockwise rotation.

Another very important aspect to consider here is your thoughts and belief system. *Whatever rotation seems most compatible with your beliefs will work best for you.* We had an opportunity to learn a healing system called *Ko-laim-ni,* which is an Atlantean healing system channeled by a group of people in West Virginia. In this system you rotate your hands clockwise to open a chakra. You then infuse light with your thoughts, and finally you rotate your hands counterclockwise to close the chakra. This system is compatible with those who perceive the chakras as rotating clockwise. When we work in this system it feels as though the chakra expands with the clockwise rotations and contracts or adjusts with the counterclockwise rotation. However, when we work in our own system our perceptions are different. We believe this example illustrates the importance of your perceptual framework and belief system in interpreting what you perceive. It is then necessary to choose what practices make sense to you and know that different ways of working with energy can be equally effective.

One other observation we have made is that once you decide

upon a certain way of directing energy with your mind, you will adapt your new energy perceptions to this current perceptual framework and understanding. For example, if you practice visualizing a circuit running from your receiving hand to your sending hand and then try to visualize it going in the opposite direction, the process may be harder and may feel uncomfortable. Once you identify the energy sense of the clearing process for yourself, you may pick up a rock and identify it as a good rock for clearing. Your new perceptions are consistent with the level in which you understand and work with energy. Someone else might not perceive the rock in that way at all. The rock, however, will still perform its balancing function, regardless of the limitations or framework we put on it. Once again we stress that *there is no single correct way of doing things.* There is room for each of our unique ways of healing ourselves and others.

CREATING ENERGY FIELDS FOR HEALING: CRYSTAL GRIDS

In addition to working actively with the energy field, it is also possible to create a healing energy field with crystals that serves as a template or perfect healing form. Powerful energy fields are created by making patterns with crystals that we call *crystal grids.* Grids maintain a steady flow of energy that merges with our human energy field as we lie receptively within its form. Using grids is one way that healing practitioners of other disciplines can amplify the healing energies inherent in those systems. In Sacred Geometry we learn that shapes have specific properties. The *triangle* is a 3 vibration, symbolizing synthesis and harmony. The inverted triangle represents the perfection of spirit in matter, and the upright triangle symbolizes the growth of matter towards spirit. The 6-pointed *Star of David* is harmony, balance, and equilibrium, represented by the interlocking triangles.

By visualizing and attuning to the Star of David form and placing crystals in this arrangement, an energy vortex is created

FIGURE 8–4. Inverted triangle, upright triangle, and Star of David.

that amplifies the balance, harmony, and perfection in our being. You can use the principles of this grid in a variety of ways.

1. We create a *Star of David Grid* with six single-pointed crystals sitting on top of pedestals (made with dowels and wood slabs) at table height, pointing inward and surrounding the healing table area. We work inside the grid. Other possibilities are to install wall shelves for these crystals, thus creating a powerful field of harmony and balance. By connecting these crystals in your mind and visualizing a Star of David before beginning your work, you will amplify the qualities of this form. Clusters can also be used for a more diffuse field. We find that the Star of David balances and expands the spiritual subtle body, so it is permanently in place in our healing room. These crystals are programmed for "continuously receiving and transmitting unconditional love, without absorbing imbalanced energies."

2. A *Double Star of David Grid* is composed of twelve crystals creating a formation that looks like the face of a clock. This is a very powerful healing grid as it steps up the process of balancing and aligning the spiritual subtle body with the other subtle bodies.

3. The *Twelve-Point Grid*, consisting of twelve crystals, is another pattern for healing work. Five pairs of crystals are

FIGURE 8–5. Star of David crystal grid.

FIGURE 8–6. Twelve-Point crystal grid.

placed just outside the major joints of the body. Crystals are placed on each side of the neck, shoulders, hips, knees, and ankles. The two remaining crystals are used to direct the flow of energy to the head and feet. Major joints often become congested with stress and tension, so crystals can play a vital role in clearing and infusing life force energy. This grid affects the etheric body because the crystals are very close to the physical body. We program crystals for this grid in the same way we program the Star of David crystals, and we clean and charge these crystals as often as necessary.

We all have a great deal to learn about sacred forms and patterns as healing tools, and crystals will play an important role in amplifying these forms of energy in the future.

9 | Self-Healing With The Three-Step Process

In this chapter we will illustrate how you can work with crystals using the three-step process for your overall well-being. We will also discuss some other possibilities for healing which you may try. The ideas included here and in the rest of the book are ones we have tried and found to be effective. Above all, *it is important for you to find your own ways of working with crystals*. Let these ideas be "seed thoughts" to get you started and to excite you into further exploration.

You can work with your thoughts using programmed crystals, or you can work on your energy field with healing crystals. Sometimes you will do a combination of both.

ATTITUDINAL HEALING WITH THE THREE STEPS

Clearing

1. You can sit in a crystal grid, using the pattern to amplify your mental work. If you have three crystals, place one behind you, and one at each knee. All three points face outward. If you have six crystals, make a Star of David with the points facing out.

2. Hold a crystal in your receiving hand with the point towards the body. You can program this crystal to bring up and release negative energy. You can also program it with the kind of music that has a soothing and cathartic effect on you. If you program a crystal to remember your dreams, it can also help you become aware of what needs to be cleared from your subconscious.

3. You can use the following visualization to contact your subconscious and to increase your awareness of what needs to be cleared:

> *Go to your favorite beautiful outdoor place . . . It is a beautiful sunny day with puffy clouds floating by . . . The sun is warm on your face and the breeze is pleasant and soothing . . . Observe this place with all your senses and feel the safety and peace that is here for you . . . Find a natural object here that appeals to you . . . Become tiny and enter it, exploring its textures, fragrances, sounds . . . While you are here ask your subconscious to give you a visual picture, sense impression, symbol, or feeling about what needs to be released . . . Ask from what area of the body the clearing needs to take place . . . Ask any other parts of your body to speak to you . . . Wait receptively and openly, knowing that you are totally safe . . . When you have received your message, come out of the natural ob-*

*ject and sit once again in your beautiful place . . . Visual-
ize the violet flame of purification or streams of water or
light cleansing and purifying you . . . Infuse the element
you have chosen to release with an affirming quality such
as patience or compassion . . . Let go . . .*

Infusing

1. Sit in the crystal grids described earlier in this chapter, with the points facing towards you.

2. Hold a special programmed crystal in your receiving hand with the point toward the body. The crystal can be programmed for self-empowerment, optimal health or other qualities you wish to affirm.

3. Here is an affirmative visualization you can use:

   *Once again, see yourself in a beautiful place . . .
   Breathe in the fragrant air . . . Notice the textures of the
   area you are standing or sitting in . . . Listen to the
   sounds . . . Gradually, you become relaxed and still in the
   peacefulness of this place . . . Call your Higher Self to be
   with you and notice the energy changes. You are surrounded with a rosy golden light of safety and unconditional Love . . . Feel the total acceptance your Higher Self
   gives you . . . See yourself surrounded by loving friends . . .
   Look into the eyes of each one . . . See how they delight in
   you . . . Hear their words of appreciation . . . In the circle
   of their love visualize yourself being and acting the way
   you wish to be . . . As each friend turns to leave, he or she
   gives you a gift, a symbol of your strength . . . When you
   are ready to leave your beautiful place, know that your
   Higher Self is always with you and that you are a precious
   flower, a delight in the world and much loved and
   appreciated . . .*

Spiritual Expansion

1. Standing in a grid, visualize its perfect form (triangle, Star of David) and the qualities it represents.

2. Open yourself to your Higher Guidance, and remain receptive. You can use a crystal programmed for contact with your Higher Self.

In practice, this three-step healing process flows and blends together, and you can move back and forth, releasing, affirming, and seeking Higher Guidance. We examine the steps mainly to illustrate and clarify how crystals can be used to amplify the process.

ENERGY FIELD HEALING WITH THE THREE STEPS

The simplest method of balancing the energy field is to follow the steps for clearing and chakra infusion given in the last chapter, using a crystal programmed for optimal well-being at all levels. This is an easy practice because it only requires one crystal.

However, we have found that a set of *seven personal chakra crystals*, each programmed for a specific chakra, can be very beneficial. We label our crystals to insure that the same crystal is always placed on the same chakra. There are several kinds of programs you can put into your chakra crystals.

1. *Chakra affirmations*: Use the affirmations from Chapter 7 or your own intuition about the meaning of each chakra. Ask the crystal to "open, balance, and expand this chakra."

2. *Sound*: Since ancient times sound has been recognized as a powerful healing and balancing energy. We have found that *each chakra resonates to a specific tone*. When you sound that tone, there is a sense of activation in the chakra area, and a

sense of energy moving up the spine as if a circuit had been connected. To find your *personal chakra tones* you will need a tuned instrument such as a piano or a pitch pipe. You can hold your pendulum, focus on your root chakra and tone middle C. Then tone C#. Watch your pendulum to see which note gives a stronger response. Sense inside your body which note seems to expand that chakra. Try the following tones:

Root: C, C#

Lower abdomen: D, D#

Solar plexus: D#, E, F

Heart: F, F#, G

Throat: G, G#, A

Third eye: A, A#

Crown: B, High C

You can use the underlined tones for general chakra expansion. The personal tones work more quickly because they are more finely tuned to your energy system.

3. *Color*: To find your *personal chakra colors*, you will need a slide projector or a sunny window, and a sample color filter set for colored gels. If you use a slide projector you can make a set of colored slides. Focus your awareness on the chakra in question. Try to have the color shining on the chakra (you can be fully clothed), and see which color gives the strongest response, just as you did with the tones. Try these colors:

Root:	*Red*, Red-orange
Lower Abdomen:	*Orange*, Gold
Solar Plexus:	Gold, *Yellow*, Green
Heart:	*Green*, Turquoise, Blue
Throat:	*Blue*, Deeper Blue, Indigo
Third Eye:	*Indigo*, Rose Purple
Crown:	*Violet*, Light Rose Lavender

These personal colors will correspond to your personal tones. Again, you can program your crystal with the underlined colors and they will work well for general expansion of a particular chakra. To program a crystal with color, mentally open the matrix of the crystal, and place it under a colored filter in the sun for a day or two. Using your pendulum, ask your crystal at the end of the first day whether it needs a second day in the sun.

Once you have programmed your set of chakra crystals, there are several ways you can work with them:

Clearing:

1. Lie in a Star of David or twelve-point grid, with the points facing out.

2. Place your programmed chakra crystals on their respective chakras, pointing toward the feet. You can place your receiving hand over each chakra, beginning with the root. Hold the crystal in your sending hand, with the point toward your fingertips. If you don't wish to use your hands, you can visualize yourself standing under a waterfall and feeling each chakra, beginning with the crown, being cleared and purified. Work with each chakra as long as you need to.

3. You can also place the chakra crystals on the body over the solar plexus, lower abdomen, and root chakras, pointing toward the feet. Place chakra crystals on the heart, throat, third eye, and crown chakras, pointing toward the head. (In the case of the crown chakra, this means pointing up above the head.) This directional system works effectively, although it will feel a little different. You can use the image of the violet flame transforming imbalanced energy at each chakra until it feels clear.

4. *Sound*: Do not place any chakra crystals on the body yet. Scan your body and find the chakras that may be deactivated. Then use your voice to go up and down the scale, like a warning siren, as high and as low as you can go. This kind of toning has the effect of freeing blocked energy. Then find a tone that seems to clear the deactivated chakra. I often find a tone between the ranges of F and A#. If you are not sure, just make a tone that seems intuitively right until you sense an energy flow in the area. *Groaning and making very loud tones can also work wonders in clearing your emotional body.* Make tones until you feel a sense of freedom, of lightness, and of being unburdened.

5. *Color*: Intuitively choose a color to visualize, like the violet flame, that feels as if it relaxes, releases, or frees you. (We use the colored slides for the infusing process rather than the clearing process at this point in time.)

Infusing

1. Lie in a Star of David or twelve-point grid, with the points facing in toward your body.

2. Place your chakra crystals on your body pointing upwards toward your head. You can hold a crystal in your receiving hand, point toward your body, and place your sending hand over your chakra. (This is the infusing position described in Chapter 8.) You can visualize white light and affirm optimal balance at each chakra.

3. *Sound*: You can hold a crystal in your sending hand, pointing out, in front of your mouth. You can then amplify your chakra tones as if you were using a crystal microphone. Beginning at your root, continue making the tone for the root until you sense that the area has received enough energy.

FIGURE 9–1. Chakra crystal layout.

Continue until you have toned all the chakras. Breathing deeply before making each tone gives you even more life force energy. You can also visualize the corresponding color at the same time.

4. *Color:* You need a slide projector and a set of color slides with the seven basic colors (or your personal colors). Place the chakra crystals on your body. Focus the slide projector on your root chakra and illuminate this chakra with the red color and breathe in red. Continue with red until you have a sense that you have had enough, and then move on to the next chakra. If you feel that you need to, you can focus the slide projector on the upper chakras after completing the lower chakras. Often, it is primarily the lower chakras that need balancing, and in our experience the color breathing helps to balance the rest of the body.

Spiritual Expansion

1. As you remain in your grid with the points facing in, attune with the qualities of that form.

2. Remain receptive to your Higher Guidance. This process is amplified by the third eye and crown chakra crystals. If you wish, you can use a small set of six crystals and place them in a Star of David above your crown. (The crown crystal is removed and the Star of David replaces it.) All points face out.

3. *Sound:* You can make your *soul tone*. To find your soul tone, work in the range above High C. My soul tone is F# above High C, an octave above my heart tone. Jonathan's soul tone is A# above High C, an octave above his third eye tone. Look for a tone that creates a current connecting you to the Earth and to your Higher Self. Your soul tone will resonate through you and feel both balancing and very expanding. It is helpful to tone your soul tone before meditation.

FIGURE 9–2. Chakra crystal layout.

4. *Color*: Visualize yourself surrounded by white light. White light contains all the colors of the spectrum and is thus very unifying. You may be aware of your *soul color*, which corresponds to your soul tone.

PLACING CRYSTALS ON THE BODY FOR SELF-HEALING

It is possible to place crystals on the body for self-healing while sleeping (or during the day), keeping several guidelines in mind. First of all, it is best to work with a mental clearing process, so that the healing process can be facilitated by the release of old beliefs. It can be helpful to place a healing crystal over an area of the body where surgery has been performed, or where you have a cut, bruise, rash, etc. In general, if the area is at the solar plexus chakra or below, you can point the crystal toward the feet and visualize a clearing taking place through the feet. If the area is at the heart or above, you can point the crystal toward the crown chakra. This is not a hard-and-fast rule, and you can point the crystal whichever way you plan to visualize the clearing process. When in doubt, ask your pendulum which way to point the crystal. Do not hesitate to change the directional flow of the crystal if conditions change in your energy field.

The other phenomenon to be aware of is an overstimulation of your energy fields, which can disrupt your sleep. Watch for jittery feelings, spontaneous jerking or twitching, or a build-up of stress in a particular area. If you feel these symptoms, try laying the crystal aside and allowing the body time to assimilate the life force energies. No two people are alike in these matters, and your beliefs about the process also influence how your body reacts. Experiment and observe yourself carefully and you will find the best ways to keep your energy at optimal levels.

QUICK ENERGIZING

As we have seen earlier, vital life force energies enter our energy field stepped-down through the chakras. Life force energies also enter through the feet and hands, and through the head, at the base of the skull and at the crown. You can place crystals on these areas to infuse energies (see illustrations). The second illustration is a more intense and concentrated infusion of energy and works well with deep breathing. Use whatever number of crystals you have, using the illustrations as suggestions.

CRYSTAL WATER

We stated earlier that our bodies are almost 70% water. The more structured the water in our bodies becomes, the more it can act as an effective semi-conductor for life force energy. Drinking crystal water is an effective way to optimize our bodily functioning. You can make crystal water by placing a crystal in a glass container, and adding spring water that you can purchase from a grocery store. Set it in the sun for a minimum of six hours or so. We use a gallon jar such as restaurants use for mayonnaise and pickles. You can try an experiment: hold your pendulum over a glass of tap water and ask to be shown the strength of the life force energy in the water. Then hold your pendulum over a glass of crystal water, asking the same question. The crystal water will probably have more life force energy. You can use your pendulum to determine how many glasses to drink each day and whether the water should be taken with herbs, homeopathic remedies, etc. Generally we drink crystal water instead of regular drinking water, and we do not take it with other remedies or medications. Heating or cooling crystal water affects the life force energy, so keep it at room temperature. You can program the crystals you use to make crystal water for optimal health at all levels.

FIGURE 9–3. Quick energizing position.

Figure 9–4. Quick energizing position.

FIGURE 9–5. Quick energizing position.

10 | Crystal Healing With Others: Level I

W HEN WORKING WITH OTHERS it is important to understand that you are *primarily a catalyst or helper, for in the end we heal ourselves.* You can enhance the optimal flow of energy in another person, but remember that the energy flow is controlled by the thoughts coming from the subconscious, conscious, and super-conscious levels. The client gains a greater sense of his power to control the attitudes necessary for healing by participating in his or her own healing through visualizations and other intuitive processes. This participation also tunes one back into one's own intuition for guidance. The healer facilitates the energy flow and assists this process by providing a safe and nuturing environment of crystal energy and healing thoughts.

In this chapter we will discuss a few simple ways that you can work with others, in addition to the ideas previously mentioned. The ideas on self-healing in Chapter 9 can also apply to working on healing others. However, it is a good idea to first become familiar with crystal energy by working on yourself. We will then describe a step-by-step energy balancing process that you can do with one to five crystals, depending on your preference. In all crystal healing work the client can be *fully clothed,* because crystal energies can be transmitted through clothing. If you decide to work otherwise, it is a matter of your own personal preference.

THE CRYSTAL PENDULUM AS A HEALING TOOL

A crystal pendulum works well to infuse color, sound, or energy into a chakra. It is best to use a crystal pendulum specifically programmed for healing rather than a pendulum used for Higher Guidance. Be certain that it has been cleaned and charged. You may have already noticed that when you first hold a crystal it feels very active, as it is releasing energy to balance with your system. Then, the crystal seems to become "quieter." In the same way, the pendulum responds through movement to correct an imbalance, becoming still when balance has been restored.

Hold the pendulum in your sending hand, three or four inches over each chakra, beginning with the root chakra. If you wish, you can hold a crystal in your receiving hand, pointing toward your body, to amplify the energy flow. *If the pendulum rotates, the area needs energy.* Continue to hold the rotating pendulum over the chakra until it becomes still. It may rotate either clockwise or counterclockwise, although one way will usually predominate. Affirm that the chakra is receiving what it needs.

If you wish to work with color, you can use a slide projector, focusing each color of the spectrum on its respective chakra. Begin with red on the root chakra. It is fascinating to watch each chakra take in varying amounts of color. Color from a slide projector affects mostly the etheric subtle body, so you can hold the pendulum about an inch and a half to two inches above the body. It takes us about twenty to thirty minutes to balance energies with color and a crystal pendulum.

IDEAS FOR MASSAGE THERAPISTS AND BODYWORKERS

1. You can work inside a crystal grid or place crystals or clusters under your healing table. You can also place crystals in the corners of the room, with the points facing the center.

2. You can tape crystals to the tops of your hands, pointing toward the fingertips, to amplify the life force energy flowing through your hands.

3. A crystal that has been rounded at one end is effective when pressed on the acupressure points and foot reflexology zones to clear blocked energy.

4. We have found that clearing blocked energy from tight muscles reduces the time necessary to massage the muscle. You first use the clearing position to restore energy flow, then massage the muscle, and finally follow with the infusing position.

5. Another clearing method that one can use at the beginning of a massage session is holding the crystal between both hands, pointing down toward the body. Roll the crystal back and forth between your hands across the body until you have covered the entire energy field.

6. To continue the clearing process, place your receiving hand on or above a congested area. Holding a crystal in your sending hand, point toward the fingertips, rotate the crystal counterclockwise in the air, away from the client's body. Continue rotating until the area feels cleared.

7. To infuse energy, hold your receiving hand in the air and hold a crystal in your sending hand, rotating it counterclockwise over the intended area, visualizing life force energy coming through the crystal into the client's body. Continue until you sense that the area has received enough energy.

FIGURE 10–1. Clearing energy.

FIGURE 10–2. Infusing energy.

CLEARING THE ENVIRONMENT

An important idea to consider is our responsibility in clearing the healing environment. First, we can sensitize ourselves to our healing room so that we know when the energies need to be purified. It is also important to acknowledge our co-creative relationship with the Devas and other spiritual beings in transforming our environment. It is part of our learning as humans to take responsibility for our actions.

1. Work with your thoughts to transform energy. First, acknowledge and thank all spiritual beings for their role in this process.

2. Before beginning a session, affirm that the energy to be cleared from a person is being transmuted and transformed. You can visualize the room filled with purifying violet light, or use another appropriate visualization.

   Another visualization you can use is bringing a white sheet up through the floor. As the sheet rises, any imbalanced energy is carried away with it. After the white sheet has passed through the room, affirm that the energies are being transformed. Taking time to do this is well worth the effort in terms of maintaining a balance in your healing environment.

3. After a session, again give thanks and acknowledgment.

4. Periodically clean and charge your healing room crystals.

5. Use sage smoke to purify the area after a healing session. Hold the container with the burning sage and walk around the room, waving the smoke into the four corners and over your healing table or area.

FURTHER COMMENTS ON HEALING

Although it is not absolutely essential, a person's trust and willingness to work with you are most helpful. However, you may find that the healing energies flowing through you are backing up into your fingers, palms, and wrists. *This is an indication that on some level the person is choosing at this time to block the flow of vital life energies.* When this happens, you have a responsibility to tell the person that it is not possible for you to do anything more for him or her at this time, and end the session. You must also release any judgmental attitudes about yourself as a healing channel, or any other negative thoughts related to the experience.

STEPS IN HEALING: LEVEL I

Crystals Used

It is helpful to have the following crystals when you begin to do crystal healing work:

1. A crystal that is programmed for optimal well-being at all levels which you hold in your sending hand. It is wise to include the protection phrase "without absorbing imbalanced energies." In the energy balancing session described below, we will call this the *hand-held crystal.*

2. A programmed crystal for the *base of the spine.* This crystal plays a role in realigning the positive-negative balance at the base of the spine, and amplifies the life force energy present there.

3. Crystals for the hands. The *receiving hand crystal* can be programmed for receiving unconditional love, optimal energy

for well-being, or intuitive guidance. The *sending hand crystal* can be programmed to release imbalanced energy through the sending hand, while amplifying the energy flow.

4. *A crystal for the base of the skull.* This is the "basic brain" area which receives energy and sends it to different parts of the body—a "circuit dispatcher area." The crystal can be programmed to receive and amplify life-giving energy.

Preparation for Healing

Take five minutes or so for the following preparations:

1. Drink crystal water.

2. Center yourself and affirm that your work is for the highest good of the client. Focus on the positive, uplifting qualities of that person, seeing them in the perfection of the Light.

3. Welcome Guides and Healing Beings of Light to work with you and through you for healing.

4. Attune to the Star of David, visualizing the client in that grid.

5. Affirm that no imbalanced energies will be absorbed, as you visualize yourself surrounded by White Light.

6. Affirm that the energy to be cleared from the person is being transmuted and transformed.

7. Attune yourself with your healing crystal.

Preparation for the Client

1. Drink crystal water.

2. Check to determine client's sending and receiving hand.

WORKING ON THE BACK

Step One—Clearing on the Back

1. The client lies on his or her stomach. Ask the client to visualize a shower of light, relaxing and purifying the body. This process can clear away some "static electricity," opening the way for greater conscious effort. The client can also practice relaxing specific parts of the back.

2. Place a crystal in the sending hand, pointing toward the fingertips.

3. Scan the back and legs with your sensing hand, about four inches from the body, for areas of blocked energy. Often, there will be blockages in the area of the adrenal glands and shoulders.

4. Roll the crystal, pointing down between your hands, over the back, to begin clearing.

5. Continue to clear blocked areas by placing your receiving hand over the area and rotating your sending hand with the crystal counterclockwise, down at your side. (This is the clearing position first described in Chapter 8.) In general, we work from the base of the spine, over both adrenals, up the back, and across the shoulders. Then we check the neck and head. If the client is using the clearing shower of light visualization, you may want to work in the direction from the head to the feet.

6. Check the energy flow in the buttocks and legs and do any clearing needed there until all clearing is completed and you can feel the energy flowing again. Often, working in one or two trouble spots, like the adrenals, will clear the energy in the back.

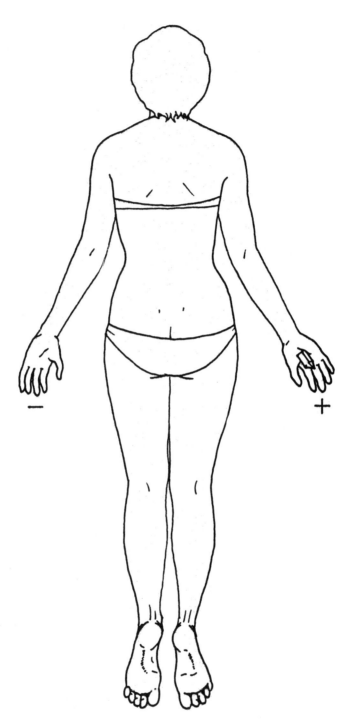

FIGURE 10-3. Clearing on the back (Level I).

7. Ask your pendulum to confirm that you have done all the clearing necessary at this time. You can also hold the pendulum over areas of the back and look for a "yes" answer, asking, "Is this area adequately cleared?"

Step Two—Infusing on the Back

1. In addition to the crystal in the sending hand, place one crystal in the receiving hand pointing toward the body, and one on the base of the spine and one at the base of the skull, both pointing toward the head.

2. During the infusion process the client can visualize energy and strength revitalizing the body. Other appropriate healing affirmations may be used, or the client may simply remain receptive and relaxed.

3. With your hand-held crystal, *infuse* energy into the base of the spine, using counterclockwise rotations, and then into the adrenals, shoulders, and any other areas where you cleared blockages. Infuse energy over the base of the skull.

4. Infuse energy into the buttocks and legs as needed.

5. After scanning with your sensing hand, check with your pendulum to see if the major areas have received the optimal amount of energy needed at this time. Working with the pendulum will help you fine-tune your perception of energy sensations until the time comes when you don't need to use it. When you are first beginning, it can help build your confidence about what you are sensing.

6. Finish evening the flow of energy in the back by making several large, circular passes around and above the body, with your hand-held crystal pointing toward the body. Move in the direction of the energy circuit in the hands. If the right hand

FIGURE 10-4. Infusing on the back (Level I).

is the receiving hand, move in a counterclockwise rotation. If the left hand is the receiving hand, move in a clockwise rotation.

7. Remove the crystals from the back and receiving hand and ask the client to turn over.

WORKING ON THE FRONT

When extensive work is done on the back, there is sometimes much less work to be done on the front. However, some people process more easily lying on their back, so sometimes we work on the front only. It is possible to do energy balancing on the front only, but it is not as thorough as work on both sides of the body.

Step One—Clearing on the Front

1. The client is holding the sending hand crystal.

2. Ask the client to dialogue with the subconscious self and find out what needs releasing, and then visualize the release process taking place.

3. Scan the body with your sensing hand as you did on the back for blocked areas.

4. Clear any blocked areas, using your hand-held crystal, until you feel the flow being restored. Check the legs after you have checked and balanced the chakras.

5. Scan with your sensing hand to check for energy flow, and confirm with your pendulum that the optimal level of clearing for this time has been done.

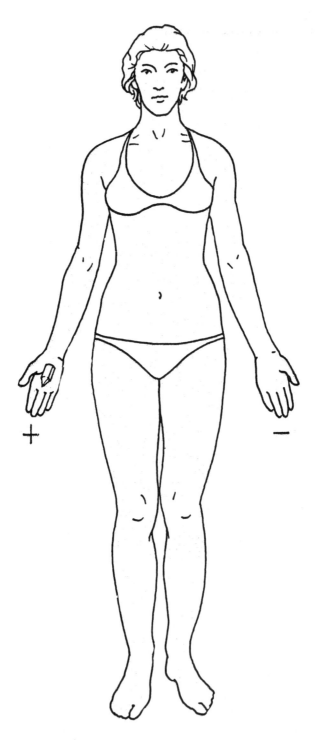

FIGURE 10–5. Clearing on the front (Level I).

Step Two—Infusing on the Front

1. Put a crystal in the client's receiving hand, in addition to the crystal in the sending hand.

2. Ask the client to visualize White Light or qualities such as courage and joy. Or the client can work with affirmations which resonate with his or her intuitive guidance. Most of all, the client can focus on self-acceptance.

3. Infuse energy with your hand-held crystal, first in the chakras where you cleared blockages, and then in any other areas where you worked. You can also work systematically up the chakras. You can use clockwise rotations at this point if you choose.

4. Rotate counterclockwise over each leg, checking for optimal energy flow. Confirm with your pendulum that each chakra is in balance.

Step Three—Spiritual Expansion on the Front

1. The client can be encouraged to attune with the Higher Self while in a state of optimal balance. This is a particularly good time to surround the client with a crystal grid.

2. You can conclude the process with any affirming thoughts that help the client to reintegrate.

Completion

1. *Any time you work with clearing energy imbalances or infusing energy for consciousness expansion, you are changing the energy pattern at each chakra as well as activating the entire energy field.* The final process of evening out the energies in

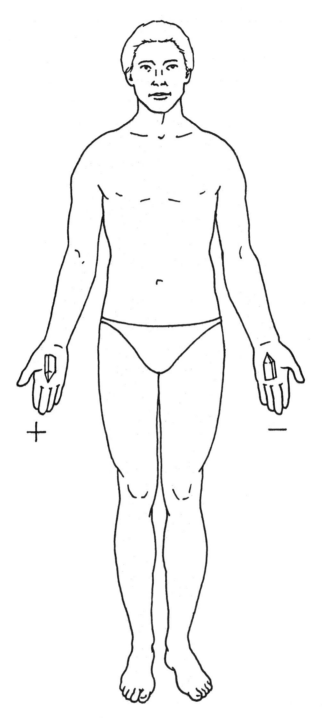

Figure 10–6. Infusing on the front (Level I).

the energy field is done to help the client function with a sense of balance in worldly affairs. Hold the crystal in your sending hand with the point facing out from your fingertips. Make several passes up the center of the client's body holding the crystal parallel to the body. Begin at the highest level that you have worked above the body, moving from the bottom of the feet to the head. Then move to a level approximately halfway between that point and the physical body. Repeat the process in the etheric body several inches above the physical body to balance the energies on that level.

2.   The next step is to affirm that each chakra is now at its optimal level of functioning for grounding and balance. Have the client begin at the crown chakra and affirm optimal functioning, while you point your hand-held crystal at each chakra, beginning with the crown chakra.

3.   Give the client time to reorient while lying on the table. Have him or her sit upright for a moment before getting off the table.

4.   If the client is still feeling dizzy, have him or her stand up while you do a *standing chakra balance*. Sometimes dizziness occurs if the client goes out of the body during a session and re-enters the body too quickly. Here are the steps for a standing chakra balance:

   a.   Stand at the side of the client with the crystal in your sending hand.

   b.   Place your receiving hand over the base of the spine and your sending hand over the root chakra. (The client is standing between your hands.)

   c.   Visualize an energy flow going from your sending hand, through your client, to your receiving hand.

   d.   Move your hands together slowly up the body. The crystal will be pointing at each chakra in turn.

   e.   At the crown chakra, touch the crystal to your receiving hand and hold the crystal pointed up above the crown.

   f.   Move your receiving hand down along the back, to the base of the spine, and gently remove your hands.

5. Encourage the client to go outdoors and take a walk or stand against a tree. Physical contact with the earth is very beneficial for the body.

6. Give the client crystal water to drink. This practice helps maintain the new level of energy.

7. Wash your hands and visualize a waterfall cleansing, purifying, and filling you with Light and Love. Appreciate your sense of Oneness with All.

8. Work with a visualization that clears the room or use some sage smoke. Clean and charge your crystals.

11 | Crystal Healing With Grids: Level II

THE STEP-BY-STEP ENERGY BALANCING described in this chapter includes additional grids for the person who would like to do more advanced crystal work. We use several different kinds of grid crystals:

1. With our largest crystals we make a *Star of David* Grid that sits on pedestals around the healing table, and we work within it. We use this grid to affect the spiritual subtle body and to provide a sacred healing energy pattern for the whole room. Therefore, crystals in this grid always point towards the center of the room. They are programmed to transmit unconditional love.

2. We form the *Twelve-Point* Grid system with crystals at the joints, and at the head and feet. We use our next largest crystals for this grid. These crystals affect the etheric subtle body, and we turn the crystals in different directions according to whether we are clearing, infusing, or expanding. They are

also programmed to "transmit optimal health at all levels without absorbing imbalanced energies."

3. We use several different sets of smaller crystals, about an inch in length, that are specifically programmed for work on the body. To avoid confusion we label these crystals according to their programs. The first set consists of the *seven chakra crystals* which we use in the infusion and spiritual expansion process.

4. Another set of crystals are for *clearing* (we have twelve). These are programmed to "restore energy flow without absorbing imbalanced energy." After some experimentation we decided that a "Y-grid" encourages energy flow in the most balanced manner. At the solar plexus and below we place them pointing toward the feet.

From the heart and upward we place them pointing toward the head.

In our experience, the triangle grid works even better for clearing than the Star of David grid on the body. We might place a single clearing crystal on a chakra or an area that is mildly congested, and the Y-grid on one or two areas where there is more blockage or deactivation.

5. We program a set of crystals (we use twelve) "to be a pure channel for well-being and consciousness expansion, without

absorbing imbalanced energies." We use these crystals for grids in the infusion and expansion process. In a chakra or an area where we want to build up energy with a focused change, we make a triangle with the chakra crystal and two expansion crystals, all pointing inward:

If we wish to infuse and expand the area we make a "Y" grid:

Sometimes at the heart or solar plexus we make a *Star of David* with one programmed chakra crystal and five expansion crystals, all pointing inward.

6. You can use these consciousness expansion crystals in a Star of David at the crown, pointing outward for spiritual expansion. They can activate movement out of the body as well as help you contact your Higher Spiritual Guidance. If you use this grid, pay extra attention to helping the client slowly integrate back into the earth plane. We use a set of *double-terminated crystals* for the crown Star of David. This seems to give a more gentle effect.

7. We have a set of thirteen crystals programmed for *color and sound* energy balancing work (with or without the slide projector). The clearing and infusing work is described in the following section on *tuning forks*.

8. In addition to the crystals that are used in grids, we will also use the crystals described in Level I. We have programmed

crystals to be used in the receiving hand for emotional clearing, forgiveness, exploring past lives, dialoguing with the physical body, and enhancing the qualities of the seven colors. We decide which crystal a client should hold, either intuitively or with a pendulum.

USING TUNING FORKS FOR SOUND HEALING

A more expensive but very potent way of working with sound in healing is to use tuning forks. You can ask your local music store to order you a set of thirteen tuning forks. Here are some ways we use them:

1. *Clearing*: Determine, either intuitively or by using your voice, a tone needed for clearing a specific area. Place a clearing crystal, corresponding color crystal, or a "Y-grid" of three clearing crystals on the area. Strike the appropriate tuning fork on a hard surface to activate the vibration. Hold the tuning fork over the crystal or in the center of the grid. You will learn to sense when the flow is restored.

2. *Infusing*: Use the personal chakra tones. Hold the appropriate tuning fork over the corresponding color crystal or a chakra crystal until the chakra has received the frequency needed. Then go to the next chakra. You can also determine the specific tone needed for any area of the body and then use the tuning fork with the appropriate color crystal or expansion crystal. The tuning fork method takes longer to learn but yields results more quickly.

3. *Clearing and Charging*: You can use tuning forks to simultaneously clear and charge crystals by placing the crystals in a circle, pointing out. One after another, going up the scale, hold each tuning fork in the center. Or you can place the crystals in an arc, and then hold the tuning fork over a crystal that points towards the arc.

WORKING WITH THE SUBTLE BODIES

If you use a room grid of some kind, you can affect the *spiritual subtle body*. When you place crystals either on or close to the body, you are affecting the *etheric subtle body*. When working with the emotional and mental subtle bodies, we do our hand rotations about four to eleven inches from the body.

Life force energy moves in toward the body from the spiritual level to the etheric level. When you are working with an imbalanced energy, you can try to sense how high above the body the imbalance begins. Then, hold your receiving hand at that level for clearing. You can infuse with your sending hand at that level also. This might mean that you are holding your hand one or two feet from the body. When you clear the imbalance at that level, the flow will be restored through the denser levels to the physical body. You can check with your sensing hand to be sure that the flow has been restored at all levels by moving it vertically toward the body. This is subtle work, and it took us some time ourselves to learn to sense energy at these levels above the body.

In the following description of a Level II Energy Balancing Session, we will repeat some of the same information that is in Level I so you will be able to follow the steps without having to constantly refer back.

STEPS IN HEALING: LEVEL II
ENERGY BALANCING WITH CRYSTAL GRIDS

Preparation for Healing

Take five minutes or so for the following preparations:

1. Drink crystal water.

2. Center yourself and affirm that your work is for the highest good of the client. Focus on the positive, uplifting qualities of that person, seeing them in the perfection of the Light.

3. Welcome Guides and Healing Beings of Light to work with and through you for healing.

4. Attune to the Star of David, visualizing the client in a Star of David light grid. You can also mentally connect your grid crystals, and amplify them with counterclockwise rotations.

5. Affirm that you are totally surrounded by White Light, and protected from any imbalanced energies.

6. Affirm that the energy cleared from the person is being transmuted and transformed, and give thanks.

7. Attune with your healing crystal.

Preparation for the Client

1. Drink crystal water.

2. Determine the client's sending and receiving hand.

WORKING ON THE BACK

Step One—Clearing on the Back

1. The client lies on his or her stomach. Ask the client to visualize a shower of light, relaxing and purifying the body. The client can also consciously relax each part of the body.

2. Use your sensing hand to scan the back and legs for areas of blocked energy. Start with your hand about four inches above the body, and check to see where the blockage begins. Now you can work at that level. Often there will be blockages in the area of the adrenal glands and shoulders.

3. A crystal can be placed in the sending hand and a twelve-point grid crystal at the bottom of the sending foot, pointing

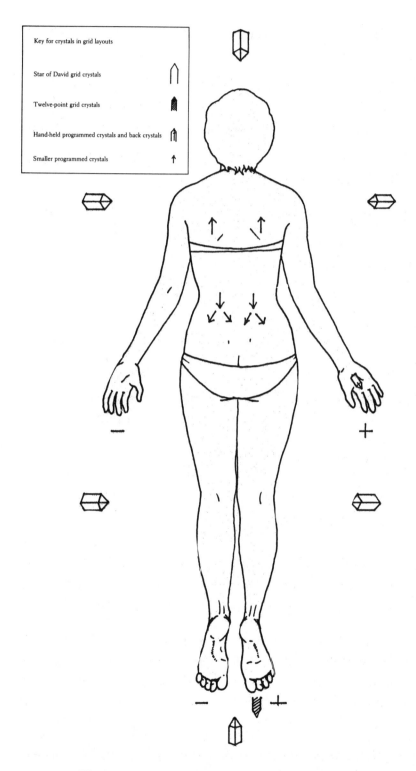

Key for crystals in grid layouts

Star of David grid crystals

Twelve-point grid crystals

Hand-held programmed crystals and back crystals

Smaller programmed crystals

FIGURE 11-1. Clearing on the back (Level II).

away from the body. You can also place the other twelve-point grid crystals at the joints, facing away from the body. Often we omit the joint crystals while working on the back, because of the time it takes to lay them out and then remove them before the client turns over. This is obviously a matter of personal preference.

4. Clearing crystals can be placed in "Y-grid" patterns at the adrenals or in other areas when necessary.

5. Roll your hand-held crystal between your hands pointing down over the back, to begin clearing.

6. Clear any blocked area using your hand-held crystal. Work from the base of the spine toward the head, and focus on the adrenal glands and shoulders. However, if the client is using the shower-of-light visualization, or if it is your preference, you can work in the direction of the head to the feet.

7. Clear the buttocks and legs. Scan the field with your sensing hand and confirm with your intuition or your pendulum that you have done all the clearing needed.

8. Remove any crystals from the back.

Step Two—Infusing Energy on the Back

1. Place crystals in the receiving and sending hands, at the base of the spine, and at the base of the skull. If you used the twelve-point grid crystals at the joints, turn them toward the body. A crystal also goes at the receiving foot, pointing toward the body, and at the sending foot, pointing away from the body.

2. Place expansion crystals anywhere you used clearing crystals. You can use single crystals or make the "Y-grid," or point all three crystals inward. The latter pattern can be helpful for the adrenals because it builds up energy in this area.

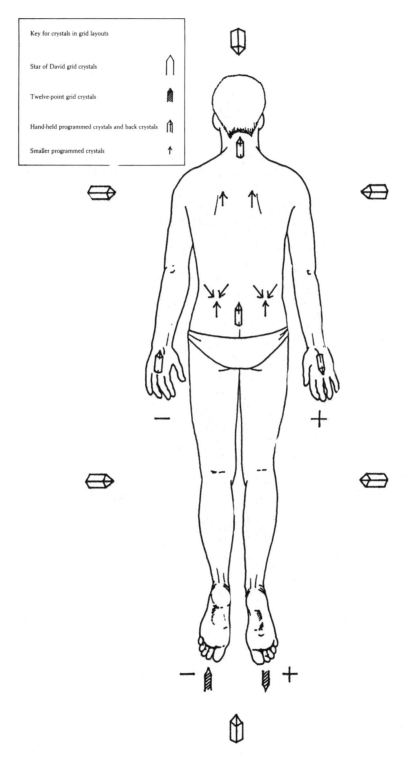

FIGURE 11-2. Infusing on the back (Level II).

3. Infuse energy into the base of the spine with your hand-held crystal using counterclockwise rotations. Move up the back and rotate over the base of the skull.

4. Infuse energy into the buttocks and legs as needed.

5. Scan with your sensing hand to see that the back has received the optimal amount of energy needed at this time. Confirm your intuition with your pendulum.

6. Finish evening the flow of energy in the back by making several large circular passes around and above the body with your hand-held crystal pointing toward the body. Move in the direction of the polarity energy circuit of the client's hands. (If the client's right hand is the receiving hand, move in a counterclockwise rotation. If the left hand is the receiving hand, move in a clockwise rotation.)

7. Remove the crystals from the back so the client can turn over. Remove the receiving hand crystal.

WORKING ON THE FRONT

Step One—Clearing on the Front

1. Ask the client to dialogue with the subconscious self and find out what needs to be released. Have the client visualize the release process taking place.

2. Scan the body for blocked areas with your sensing hand.

3. Crystals can be placed in the sending hand and at the bottom of the sending foot, pointing away from the body. Place the twelve-point grid crystals at the joints, facing away from the body. One crystal can go above the head, pointing up.

4. Clearing crystals can be placed in "Y-grids" on deactivated chakras, or singly wherever needed.

Key for crystals in grid layouts

Star of David grid crystals

Twelve-point grid crystals

Hand-held programmed crystals and back crystals

Smaller programmed crystals

FIGURE 11–3. Clearing on the front (Level II).

5. Clear any blocked areas, using a hand-held crystal, until you feel the flow being restored. Begin with the most deactivated chakra, and then work down to the root and then up to the crown. Check the legs after you check the chakras.

6. Scan for restored energy flow with your sensing hand. Confirm with your intuition or your pendulum that you have done the clearing needed on the front.

Step Two—Infusing on the Front

1. Place a crystal in the receiving hand. Turn the twelve-point grid crystals toward the body for a build-up of energy. Decide either intuitively or with your pendulum whether the grid crystal at the head needs to point toward the head or away from the head. When the crystal is pointing toward the head, the infusion is very focused and intense. Most often we point the crystal upward, away from the head. The crystal at the sending foot can be moved to a position between the feet and pointing upward to direct the energy flow. It can also be placed at the receiving foot pointing towards the body to amplify the life force energy coming through the receiving foot.

2. Ask the client to visualize White Light, qualities such as courage and joy and affirmations appropriate to his or her intuitive nature. Most of all, the client can focus on self-acceptance.

3. Place expansion or chakra crystals where you used clearing crystals. You can make "Y-grids" to infuse and spread the energy, or you can point all crystals inward to build up energy in a specific area.

4. Infuse energy with your hand-held crystal, rotating either clockwise or counterclockwise, first in the chakras where you cleared blockages, and then in any other areas where you

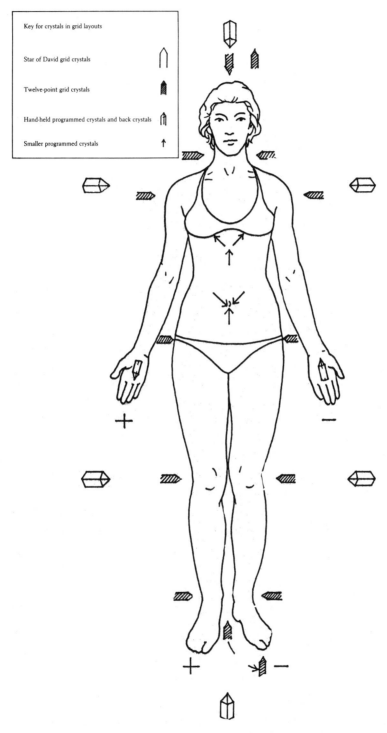

Key for crystals in grid layouts

Star of David grid crystals

Twelve-point grid crystals

Hand-held programmed crystals and back crystals

Smaller programmed crystals

FIGURE 11–4. Infusing on the front (Level II).

worked. Check each chakra with counterclockwise rotations, beginning with the root chakra, to make sure each is optimally balanced.

5. Scan with your sensing hand and confirm, either intuitively or with a pendulum, that the front of the body has received the energy it needs.

Step Three—Spiritual Expansion on the Front

1. Turn the twelve-point grid crystals parallel to the body according to the polarity circuit of the hands. On the receiving-hand side the crystals point up towards the head, and on the sending-hand side they point down towards the feet. A crystal remains between the feet, and another above the head, both pointing up. This pattern maintains a balanced flow of energy in the body.

2. The client if encouraged to attune with his or her Higher Self while in this state of optimal balance.

3. Place the seven chakra crystals on the body.

4. You can remove the crown chakra crystal and the twelve-point grid crystal above the head, and replace them with expansion crystals in a Star of David grid pattern with the points out.

5. You can conclude the process with silence, or with any affirming thoughts that reintegrate or reconnect.

6. Even the energies throughout the energy field by making several passes up the center of the client's body, holding the crystal parallel to the body. Begin at the highest level where you have worked above the body, moving from the bottom of the feet to the head. Then move to a level approximately halfway between that point and the physical body. Finally,

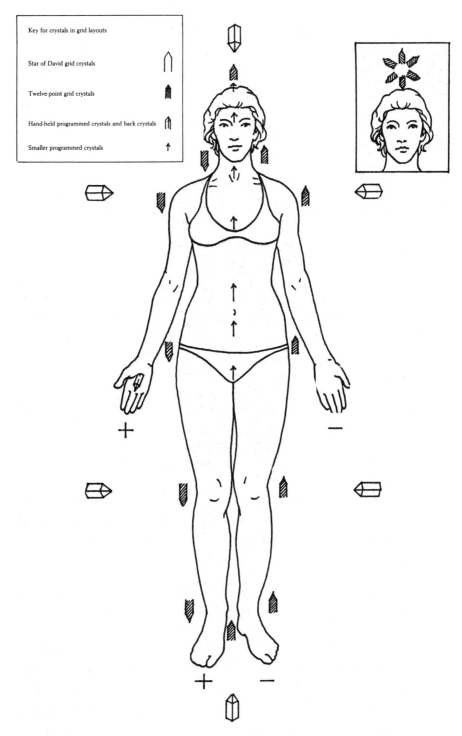

FIGURE 11–5. Spiritual expansion on the front (Level II).

repeat the process in the etheric body, several inches above the physical body and even the energies on that level.

Completion

1. Remove all crystals on and around the body.

2. The next step is to affirm that each chakra is now at its optimal level of functioning for grounding and balance. Have the client affirm optimal functioning of each chakra, beginning at the crown chakra, while you simultaneously point your hand-held crystal at that chakra.

3. Give the client time to reorient while lying on the table. Have him or her sit upright before getting off the table.

4. Ask the client to stand. If the client is still feeling dizzy, do a *standing chakra balance*. Sometimes this happens if the client "leaves the body" during a session and re-enters the body too quickly. Here are the steps for a standing chakra balance:

    a. Stand at the side of the client with the crystal in your sending hand.

    b. Place your receiving hand over the base of the spine. Place your sending hand over the root chakra.

    c. Visualize an energy flow going from your sending hand, through your client, to your receiving hand.

    d. Move your hands together slowly up the body. The crystal will be pointing at each chakra in turn.

    e. At the crown chakra, touch the crystal to your receiving hand and hold the crystal pointed up above the crown.

    f. Move your receiving hand down along the back to the base of the spine, and gently remove your hands.

5. Encourage the client to go outdoors and take a walk or stand against a tree. Contact between the earth and the physical body is very beneficial.

6. Give the client crystal water to drink. This practice helps one to maintain the new level of energy. The client may want to discuss his or her experiences.

7. Wash your hands, visualizing a waterfall cleansing, purifying, and filling you with Light and Love. Appreciate your sense of Oneness with All.

8. Work with a visualization that clears the room or use some sage smoke. Clean and charge your crystals.

12 | Planetary Healing

I<small>N</small> C<small>HAPTER</small> 1 <small>WE EXPLAINED</small> how everything is composed of life force energy. All forms in the physical universe are complex, organized patterns of life force energy. As you begin to work with crystals you will realize that life force energy is *conscious energy*. In fact, in many Eastern traditions this all-pervading creative energy is called *Consciousness*. In these traditions Consciousness and life force energy are understood to be inseparable—like two sides of the same coin. One cannot exist without the other.

It is the nature of Consciousness to exist in a state of inter-connectedness and constant evolution. Everything in the universe exists at varying levels of Consciousness. On a physical level, Consciousness is the harmonious interaction of each cell and molecule to maintain the balance of the whole. On a spiritual level, we experience Consciousness as unconditional love, balance, harmony, and peace, as well as a constant process of change. Human beings, quartz crystals, and everything else in Nature have their own individual Consciousness that evolves toward the fulfillment of its pattern of growth, on both the physical and spiritual levels. In the following channelings, the Crystal Deva elaborates on this theme:

''As the Human Kingdom grows through life's experiences and through changes of physical vehicles, I too am evolving, for I was created from the same spark of energy as was the Human Kingdom. I retain and store knowledge within my being just as the Human Kingdom stores memory. You see, my capacity for storing knowledge is infinitely greater than that of the Human Kingdom, because the Human Kingdom has chosen to perceive itself as more limited in different ways. Creative expression is a vitally important aspect of my work and is important at this time, for I am a catalyst to help pull the Human Kingdom out of its limits, to see a greater reality, to enable humanity to tap into the far reaches of the infinite cosmos. . . . ''

We can learn much about unconditional love and other qualities such as patience and trust by attuning with Nature's Kingdoms.

''I have the ability to instill confidence and courage in all who choose to work with me, for where there is even a seed of those qualities, I have the capacity to expand them within you to their highest ultimate form. Know that it is impossible to hate or fear when you have come into pure connection with me, for I am a channel of pure unconditional Love and Light for the Human Kingdom as well as all other Kingdoms. (That is why my energies are so well received by the Plant Kingdoms.) I can enable you to speak with pure truth, with clarity and understanding in all situations and experiences that unfold in life. . . . ''

Each crystal has a higher purpose to serve which can be ascertained either by sitting receptively with the crystal and attuning with it or by using a pendulum. Although there are some sources which classify crystals according to their function, we find that you can limit the wisdom crystals can teach you by imposing a set of characteristics or descriptions upon them. Here are some questions that can help you receive intuitive guidance about a crystal's purpose.

1. "Is your highest function to restore harmony and balance on the physical, emotional, or mental levels of my being?" (Healing)

   a. "Can you be placed on the physical body?"

   b. "Are you to work with clearing negative thoughts?"

2. "Is your highest function to expand the light within my Higher Spiritual Levels?" (Meditation)

3. "Is your highest purpose related to Planetary Healing?"

4. "Is it for your highest good to be used for Devic or other interdimensional communication?"

5. "Do you have stored symbols or other knowledge inside you to be accessed receptively?"

6. "Is it for your highest good to be used in a technological capacity or in a grid system as a transmitter?

Above all, it is important to remember that any time you work with a crystal to assist your spiritual growth, or to be of service to others, you are fulfilling both your own higher purpose and that of the crystal.

PLANETARY HEALING

Consciousness or life force energy is our very life. We are both made of it and sustained by it. It is important to recognize our interconnectedness with the whole spectrum of life force energies, from the earth's geomagnetic energy field to Higher

Spiritual Consciousness. We need food, air, and water to live. We also need the nourishment of love in order to live—a love that is based on a balance of giving and receiving. As we learn to express our interconnectedness and love in more and more ways, we evolve and make many changes in this process. We change as we explore different levels of knowledge. We learn that the quality of our thoughts and actions affects our own life, the lives of others, and the planet as well, since *we are the Earth and the Earth is us.* And so Planetary Healing becomes a way of life, because Planetary Healing is life.

In this book we have focused on how transforming our thoughts changes the quality of the life force energy that we receive and utilize in our personal healing. Working with our thoughts is a form of Planetary Healing, because the life force energy expressed in our thoughts becomes part of the life energy, or Consciousness, that sustains the physical and spiritual aspects of our planet. In the following channelings, the Crystal Deva talks about the Devic Kingdom and how the Devas work with thought forms:

> ''My Kingdom is based in the world of Spirit. We Devas have no physical structure as you do. We are 'Light Beings' with light bodies that are essentially formless. Our will is the Will of the Divine, whereas you have both a personal will and the Higher Will of the Divine. You communicate primarily on the verbal level where we utilize thought based in pure knowingness. You have a powerful effect on your earth plane reality since you live within a physical vehicle, on the earth plane. You work with the physical form of things. We operate in the realm of life force energies that are without physical structure. Our purpose is to create the reality of physical form through our work with life force energies. In our dimension time and space are infinite. Everything *Is.* We communicate directly with Infinite Light and Wisdom. It is the same as

your being at one with your Higher Self Essence. We seek a greater expansion and knowingness of spirit, as you do. We work without emotional considerations of our actions, knowing that we are eternally linked to the Light. . . .

''I am a Deva for the clear crystal blueprint. There are also overlighting Devas that create the blueprint of balance for a geographical area. The size of the area is determined by the number of different life forms involved, and the extent that we receive human cooperation in maintaining balance.

''We work to maintain balance within the life forms that have been created physically on or within the earth's surface. We continue to transmit new energized forms that are created from life force energy.

''Positive human thought forms increase the quality of life force energy that permeates the elements of the Planet. This results in normal, healthy growth cycles for all of Nature's Kingdoms. We do not rely solely on positive human thought energies in our work. But the more positive the energy that has been transmitted from the Human Kingdom, the more we can sustain the existing balance of energy on the Planet.

''When we are aware of a negative human group thought form, we surround it with White Light so that no further expansion of that thought form can take place. We then focus light towards its center to transform its energies into a neutralized state. We also begin work at the outer layers of the form, again with focused White Light. Change takes place as the layers take on greater light. Once the thought form has been totally neutralized, then the encircling light is removed because it is no longer needed. The form is charged with life force energies by imprinting a perfect pattern on it, and then it is transmitted for use in Planetary balance.

''We also work in an orderly manner with each positive group thought form, such as the ones created on December 31, and on the solstices and equinoxes. We sense its different vibrational levels, or layers, to determine where the energy can be optimally utilized by the Planet. We then accompany each vibrational level to its destination and infuse its light into the appropriate energy field for healing and balance.

''Not every group thought form is dispersed throughout the entire planet. We have maintained the positive group thought form energies manifested at the time of the Harmonic Convergence according to the Higher Guidance that we receive. Its presence serves as a 'guiding light channel' for those of the Human Kingdom that are moving into higher levels of Consciousness.''

USING CRYSTALS FOR PLANETARY HEALING

There are several ways you can use crystals for Planetary Healing:

1. When working individually, you can hold a crystal and see Planet Earth as totally healed and vibrantly alive, with all her kingdoms in perfect order and balance. This thought will merge with others of similar vibrational frequency, and the crystal will also amplify your thoughts. It is not so much the particular thought content, but the *quality of your compassion* that makes the difference.

2. When you decide to go to a natural area, take quartz crystal with you. It comes from the Earth and feels right at home. Through your thoughts send unconditional love to the Kingdoms of Nature around you. Your thoughts can be used to help balance the natural area you are in.

3. The veins of quartz crystal serve a significant function in transforming and stabilizing the energies that flow from the earth's core to the surface. In many locations quartz crystal is being mined without consideration for the imbalance it may be creating in Mother Earth.

   Merge with your crystal and visualize yourself in a cave with myriads of beautiful crystal clusters and points . . . Travel through the cave, feeling the balance and clarity of the crystals . . . The cave stretches on to become veins of crystal under the earth . . . Visualize waves of balanced, clear crystal energy flowing like light through the veins, spreading under the surface of the earth . . .

4. Consider working with a group for Planetary Healing. You can do a healing meditation in which each person holds a crystal in the sending hand and focuses healing thoughts to a crystal grid or a single crystal in the center. The center crystal can represent the Earth, and it will also amplify the power of group focus.

5. We have also used a world map as a way of focusing energy. Each person can hold a crystal in the sending hand for amplification, and place another crystal on the map where he or she wishes to send healing energy. You can also place crystals on sacred places like the pyramids in Egypt. Each person focuses healing energy and peace to a particular spot in the world, and then to the Planet as a whole.

   "Humans as a group are going to recognize that the life force energy that maintains their existence is a most sacred resource. Open your total being to the healing process whether you are the giver or the receiver. Be creative with the ways that you work with clear quartz crystal. Be patient, and open to her teachings as she shares the wisdom of life with you."

FOOTNOTES

Chapter 1:

1. Kenneth Cohen, "Bones of Our Ancestors," *Yoga Journal* 60 (1985), p. 56.

2. Judith Larkin, Ph.D., "Counseling With Crystals," in John Vincent Milewski and Virginia L. Harford, eds., *The Crystal Sourcebook* (Santa Fe: Mystic Crystal Publications, 1987), pp. 263–265.

3. Ibid., p. 266.

4. Edmund Harold, *Focus on Crystals* (New York: Ballantine Books, 1986), p. 5.

5. Ibid., pp. 9–10.

6. John Vincent Milewski, Ph.D., "Herkimer Diamonds," in John Vincent Milewski and Virginia L. Harford, eds., *The Crystal Sourcebook* (Santa Fe: Mystic Publications, 1987), p. 217.

Chapter 3:

1. Randall Baer and Vicki Baer, *Windows of Light* (New York: Harper & Row, 1984), p. 60.

Chapter 4:

1. Albert Roy Davis and Walter C. Rawls, Jr., *Magnetism and Its Effects on the Living System* (Hicksville: Exposition Press, 1974), p. 23.

Chapter 6:

1. Gabriel Cousens, M.D., *Spiritual Nutrition and the Rainbow Diet* (Boulder: Cassandra Press, 1986), p. 37.

2. Ibid., p. 49.

3. Ibid., p. 81.

4. Ibid., p. 89.

5. Randall Baer and Vicki Baer, *The Crystal Connection* (New York: Harper & Row, 1986), p. 343.

6. Aubrey Westlake, *The Pattern of Health* (New York: Devin-Adair Co., 1963), p. 35.

7. Ibid., p. 36.

Bibliography

Alper, the Reverend Dr. Frank. *Exploring Atlantis, Vols. I and II.* Phoenix: Arizona Metaphysical Society, 1982.

Baer, Randall N., and Vicki B. *Windows of Light.* New York: Harper & Row Publishers, Inc., 1984.

Baer, Randall N., and Vicki B. *The Crystal Connection.* New York: Harper & Row Publishers, Inc., 1986.

Burke, George. *Magnetic Therapy.* Oklahoma City: Saint George Press, 1980.

Lantieri, Linda, and Elaine Seiler. *Quartz Crystal, A Gift From the Earth.* Northhampton: Resource Management Ltd., 1985.

Logan, Elizabeth A. *A Crystal Cosmos Network Directory.* Winnipeg: Crystal Cosmos Network, 1986.

Milewski, John Vincent, and Virginia L. Harford. *The Crystal Sourcebook.* Santa Fe: Mystic Crystal Publications, 1987.

Nielson, Greg, and Joseph Polasky. *Pendulum Power.* New York: Warner Books, 1977.

Raphaell, Katrina. *Crystal Enlightenment.* New York: Aurora Press, 1985.

Small, Jacqueline. *Transformers, the Therapists of the Future.* Marina del Rey: De Vorss and Company, 1982.

Walker, Dael. *The Crystal Book.* Sunol: The Crystal Company, 1983.

Westlake, Aubrey. *The Pattern of Health.* New York: Devon-Adair Co., 1963.

Further Information and Training

Jonathan and Pamela are available for workshops on Crystals and Crystal Healing. Write:

Johathan Pawlik and Pamela Chase
2004 Porta Court NW
Olympia, WA 98502

or

Johathan Pawlik and Pamela Chase
c/o Newcastle Publishing Company
P.O. Box 7589
Van Nuys, CA 91409

A *Crystal Cosmos Network Directory* carries a national listing of people involved in crystal healing, teaching, and research. It also lists sources for crystals, jewelry, and supplies. The directory is updated about once every two years. Write:

Elizabeth A. Logan
Crystal Cosmos Network
Box 2386
Winnipeg, Manitoba
Canada R3c 4A6

The Crystal Sourcebook, edited by John Milewski and Virginia Harford, gives an extensive bibliography on crystals and stones. It lists sources for crystals, as well as some teachers and researchers. Write:

Mystic Crystal Publications
P.O. Box 8029
Santa Fe, New Mexico 87504

To obtain a sample pack of color filters ($3\frac{1}{4}$" × $1\frac{1}{2}$" × 1"), contact the following:

Rosco	or	Rosco
36 Bush Ave.		1135 North Highland Ave.
Port Chester, N.Y. 10573		Hollywood, CA 90038